Praise for The Way of Eating

"Like everyone else with a serious interest in Chinese food, I've long heard rumors of Yuan Mei and his seminal book. Alas, there was no English translation. Now there is—and it's even better than anticipated. This is far more than a cookbook: The Way of Eating is food history at its finest, a window into a fascinating and long-lost world."

——**Ruth Reichl**, author of Save Me the Plums

"The publication of The Way of Eating: Yuan Mei's Manual of Gastronomy is indeed a landmark event and not only in culinary scholarship. Yuan's wit and love of food is an added bonus and greatly enhances our understanding of one of the world's greatest cuisines."

—**Ken Hom**, OBE, author of My Stir-fried Life and other cookery books

"The Way of Eating is one of China's greatest classical cookbooks. It is also unique in that it beguiles its readers with wit, intelligence, and brevity, much like Fernand Point's Ma Gastronomie. Translating something as difficult as this is therefore an event worth celebrating, and kudos go out to Sean Chen for his meticulously scholarly approach. Open the cover and prepare to be enchanted."

—**Carolyn Phillips**, author of All Under Heaven

"Finally: a lively, scholarly, and usefully-annotated English translation of Yuan Mei's seminal cookbook and culinary treatise that captures the spirit of the original work. Sean Chen and the Berkshire team have performed a great service for the world of gastronomy by making this fascinating text accessible to English-speaking readers."

— **Fuchsia Dunlop**, author of Land of Fish and Rice and other cookery books

"This new translation of Yuan Mei's legendary book is cause for celebration, not only because the complete text is finally available in English, but because Sean Chen so beautifully captures the author's lyricism, humor, and opinionated pronouncements. Reading this book is like sitting down to a meal with a charming dinner partner whose interests range from culinary technique to aesthetics to the nature of hospitality, though flavor always remains foremost for him. This volume shares the delights and concerns of one of the world's most artful gastronomes, and in the process offers a fascinating look at eighteenth-century Chinese culture."

— **Darra Goldstein**, founding editor of Gastronomica: The Journal of Food and Culture

"The Way of Eating is a classic and two centuries later it still sparkles with Yuan's irascible charm, his epic passion for food, and his near-religious devotion to the pleasures of the senses."

—**Nicole Mones**, author of the novel The Last Chinese Chef

THE WAY
OF
EATING

YUAN MEI'S MANUAL OF GASTRONOMY

THE WAY
OF
EATING

YUAN MEI'S MANUAL OF GASTRONOMY

TRANSLATED AND ANNOTATED BY
SEAN J. S. CHEN
FOREWORD BY NICOLE MONES
EDITORIAL ADVISORS E. N. ANDERSON
AND JEFFREY RIEGEL

LⱢⱢ BERKSHIRE

Digital editions. *The Way of Eating* is available through most major e-book and database services (please check with them for pricing).

Bilingual (English and Chinese) edition published as *Recipes from the Garden of Contentment*.

For information, contact

Berkshire Publishing Group
122 Castle Street
Great Barrington, Massachusetts 01230-1506 USA
Email: info@berkshirepublishing.com
Tel: +1 413 528 0206
Fax: +1 413 541 0076

Publisher: Karen Christensen
Editor: Marjolijn Kaiser
Copyeditors: Kathy Brock & Olette Trouve
Illustrator: Lichia Liu
Compositor: Amnet Systems
Cover image by Karen Christensen: Imitation Pheasant prepared by chef Nick Liu During the launch party at the University of Toronto Scarborough.

Library of Congress Cataloging-in-Publication Data

Names: Yuan, Mei, 1716-1798. | Chen, Sean Jy-Shyang, translator. | Mones, Nicole, writer of foreword.

Title: The way of eating : Yuan Mei's manual of gastronomy / by Yuan Mei ; translated by Sean J. S. Chen ; foreword by Nicole Mones.

Other titles: Sui yuan shi dan. English

Description: Great Barrington, MA : Berkshire Publishing Group, 2019. | English. |

Identifiers: LCCN 2019003831 (print) | LCCN 2019008440 (ebook) | ISBN 9781614728269 | ISBN 9781614728276 (pbk.) | ISBN 9781614728283 (hardcover)

Subjects: LCSH: Cooking, Chinese—Early works to 1800. | Food habits—China—Early works to 1800.

Classification: LCC TX724.5.C5 (ebook) | LCC TX724.5.C5 Y822613 2019 (print) | DDC 641.5951--dc23

LC record available at https://lccn.loc.gov/2019003831

Table of Contents

Foreword

Nicole Mones, author of The Last Chinese Chef *and other novels*

While he lived, Yuan Mei 袁枚 (1716–1798) was China's most important literary figure; more than two-hundred years after his death, he is still considered one of the two or three greatest poets of the eighteenth century. In China, where poetry has traditionally been the most exalted literary form, this is fame of a high order. Yet outside China, he is popularly known not for his poetry but for authoring a seminal work on Chinese food, which is revered by Chinese chefs, but has never, until now, been published in English.

It may seem odd that a celebrity poet and Qing dynasty bureaucrat ended up producing China's greatest food classic, but Yuan Mei was an obsessive and fanatical diner. He lived by his profound belief that life's sensual pleasures—including food—were gifts of nature, meant to be fully enjoyed and appreciated, and that to disdain such gifts was an affront to heaven. So throughout his life, whenever he tasted a standout dish at someone else's home, he sent his cook over to learn how to make it, and then recorded the procedure, alongside his thoughts. He spent years organizing this material into a book, working on it "in the intervals of writing poetry" (Waley 1956, 195), as he put it, circulating the manuscript among his friends. It was finally completed and printed in 1792—a systematic and fairly comprehensive guide to preparing a wide range of foods, spiced with Yuan's delightfully opinionated asides.

No such food book had ever been widely circulated in China. Chinese cookery was historically taught through apprenticeship rather than books, and since the position of a chef in feudal China, whether in a restaurant or private home, was a lowly one, many were illiterate. Naturally that did not stop men of letters such as Lu Yu 陸羽, Su Dongpo 蘇東坡, and Li Liweng李笠翁[1] from writing about how food, wine, and tea should be appreciated, any more than it stopped dedicated foodies (such as Yuan Mei) from sitting down in their homes and organizing all they had learned about cooking into a book. Multiple such family cookbooks survive, one of the oldest being Madame Wu's Song dynasty compilation, A *Housewife's Handbook* (also known as *Madame Wu's Recipe Book*), roughly a thousand years old. So Yuan Mei was not the only Chinese thinker to obsess about food for a lifetime and then write down his findings and opinions. But such was his talent and celebrity, so sterling were his tastes and standards—indeed, his admonitions against dining as a display of wealth seem more relevant than ever today—that *The Way of Eating* endured. It has been widely accepted as the first great gathering of Chinese culinary knowledge.

It was not the last, however. In researching my novel *The Last Chinese Chef*, which contains a faux Chinese food classic, I was thrilled by later books which genuinely deepened and expanded Yuan Mei's accomplishment—notably, in English, the magisterial *Chinese Gastronomy* (1969) by Hsiang Ju Lin and Tsuifeng Lin. Still, *The Way of Eating* is the classic, and two centuries later, it still sparkles with Yuan's irascible charm, his epic passion for food, and his near-religious devotion to the pleasures of the senses.

One might almost say that the veneration of earthly pleasures is the closest thing Yuan Mei had to a religion. Without doubt, he had little time for Buddhism, which taught that sensual joys were dissolute; neither did he respond to Confucianism, which dictated that poetry should be for moral instruction, not personal expression—the opposite of his own ideas. In a similar vein, Yuan did not enjoy bureaucracy, and although as a presented scholar degree-holder (*jinshi* 進士) and member of the elite Hanlin Academy he was obliged to hold a series of posts (eventually landing him in Nanjing), he chafed at the official life. In his mid-thirties, he

---

1 Lu Yu (733–804) is the author of the Tang dynasty book The Classic of Tea 茶經. Su Dongpo (1037–1101), also known as Su Shi 蘇軾, was a Song dynasty writer, poet, and gastronome. Li Liweng (1611–1680) was a Qing dynasty writer and publisher, well-known for his novel *The Carnal Prayer Mat* (*Rou putuan* 肉蒲團). Besides these famous figures, Yuan Mei also refers to Ni Zan 倪瓚 (1301–1374) and Xu Wei 徐渭 (1521–1593), two gastronomes from the Yuan and Ming dynasties respectively.

decided to leave his post permanently, retire, and give his life over to poetry and food. "All I ask for is a village of some ten houses where I could live exactly as I chose, and rule the people merely by chanting to them the Way of the Former Kings; then I could end my days there in perfect contentment, even though I only ranked as a village constable...all I ask for is to be able to take such a rest, and you ought not to blame me" (Waley, 47).

Now that he'd given up his job with its official residence, Yuan needed a new home. To his joy he found a steep, uneven, wildly overgrown piece of land that had been deserted for years, except for one building having been used as a tavern. Yuan fell in love with it. He paid three hundred ounces of silver for it, named it Suiyuan 随园 (Garden of Contentment), built his home there, and remained for the rest of his life. It was his anchor and his refuge. Along with his near-spiritual passion for food, the garden itself was the other creative force behind the book.

The place needed a tremendous amount of work, but he was in no hurry and besides, he wanted to help re-fashion the grounds himself:

> The work on my garden may never be finished, my expenditure on it may well prove beyond my means. Very well then; some things that are lacking will have to wait till they can be supplied; some things that are broken will have to wait until they can be repaired. There is no fixed time by which anything has to be done. Whatever happens I shall be better off than in old days when I had to be all the time bowing and scraping to jacks-in-office. I am just thirty-seven. I am determined to settle here. Whether I can make something of this place and live in it permanently only the future can decide. (Waley, 69)

When he was done, his home boasted twenty-four pavilions, and a miniature replica of the famous West Lake in Hangzhou (his birthplace), complete with a causeway and small arched bridges.

But to produce the food of Yuan Mei's dreams, his home needed a master chef, and fate complied by sending him the extraordinary Wang Xiaoyu 王小余. This was a remarkable man, and Yuan's prose shows it:

> When he first came, and asked what was to be the menu for the day, I feared that he had grand ideas, and I explained to him that I came

of a family that was far from rich and that we were not in the habit of spending a fortune for every meal. "Very good," he said, laughing, and presently produced a vegetable soup that was so good that one went on and on taking it till one really felt one needed nothing more...He insisted on doing all the marketing himself, saying, "I must see things in their natural state before I can decide whether I can apply my art to them." At the stove, he capered like a sparrow, but never took his eyes off it for a moment, and if when anything was coming to boil someone called out to him, he took not the slightest notice, and did not even seem to hear...I once asked him why, when he could easily have got a job in some affluent household, he had preferred to stay all these years with me in the Sui Garden. "To find an employer who appreciates one is not easy," he said, "but to find one who understands anything about cookery is harder still. The ordinary hard-drinking revelers at a fashionable dinner party would be equally happy to gulp down any stinking mess. You, on the contrary, continually criticize me, abuse me, fly into a rage with me, but on every such occasion make me aware of some real defect; so that I would a thousand times rather listen to your bitter admonitions than to the sweetest praise...Say no more! I mean to stay on here." (Waley, 52–53)

This conversation exposes one of the fascinating linchpins of Chinese gastronomy: the gourmet is as important as the chef. At its highest levels, Chinese cuisine is so subtle and so resonant that an aware and receptive diner is absolutely critical to the exchange—so that in China, it is actually possible for a gourmet to be as renowned as a chef. Without question Yuan Mei was one of the premier gourmets in Chinese history, and Wang Xiaoyu, for the ten years they had together before Wang died, was his culinary soulmate.

But Yuan Mei's friends were also part of his lifelong food quest, since he traveled extensively with them, memorializing great meals along the way, and also dined—and collected recipes, as these pages attest—in their homes. He had many friends; on his eightieth birthday, he received over three thousand letters and poems of congratulation. He also seems to have been a great friend himself—generous, lovable, steadfast, smart, and fun. Witness this description of a typical evening with Jiang Hening 蔣和寧 (1709–1768), his friend for fifty years: "We were neither of us drinkers and both of us were fond of talking about the past. We trimmed the candles and sat opposite one another, discussing the ups and downs of national affairs during the last three thousand years, appraising all the outstanding figures and, when we found ourselves in particularly close agreement on some disputed point, thumping on our stools and shouting with delight, even more pleased with each other than before" (Waley, 26).

Throughout his life Yuan Mei was so alive to the pleasures of the mind, of poetry, of cuisine...could a man like him possibly say no to love, that other sublime gift of nature? Certainly not. He had a reputation. His older friend and mentor Shi Yizhi 史貽直 (1682–1763) wrote to him, "I hear that you have been doing very well in your post at Nanjing, but that you do not 'avoid the frivolity of Tu [Du] Mu.'" A poet of the Tang dynasty, Du Mu 杜牧 (803–852) loved his concubines and singing girls, as did Yuan Mei (Waley, 60).

He had a wife, multiple concubines, and written sources document at least one waiting-her-time-girl (a female child acquired to become a concubine later). He once took as concubine a friend's servant girl, after their eyes met in a certain way. On observing it, the friend made Yuan Mei a gift of the girl. Along these same lines, don't miss his enthusiasm for "Xiao the beauty," a street vendor, in this book's section on appetizers.

Crazy about women, Yuan also had deep relationships with men. He maintained bromances for decades, going on long journeys of many months with his companions, and keeping up literary and personal exchanges with them throughout his life. And though he was never interested in men to the exclusion of women, he did have an eye for good-looking young male actors. His account of the time he spent at age twenty-three with the handsome boy actor Xu Yunting, to whom he later addressed oblique poems, illuminates his omnivorous nature:

All the Hanlin scholars were crazy about him and clubbed together to pay for theatricals in which he appeared. I was young and good-looking, but I was so poorly accoutred that I did not think Yun-t'ing [Yunting] could possibly find me worth cultivating. But I noticed on one occasion that he often glanced my way and smiled, quite with the air of indicating that he had taken a fancy to me. I hardly dared to believe this and did not try to get in touch with him.

However, very early next day I heard a knock at my door. There he was; and we were soon on the most affectionate terms—a state of affairs all the more delightful, because it far exceeded anything I had expected. (Waley, 27)

By midlife, Yuan was well off; he could earn as much as a thousand ounces of silver for a single tomb inscription, though his usual pay was about half that, still a rich income. In position to do what he liked, and perhaps feeling he had not yet done enough to rattle straight-laced society, he started teaching poetry to women. Soon he had a long line of beautiful, intelligent students he called his "moth-eyebrow academy." Teaching females to read and write was actually not outrageous in eighteenth-century China, for many members of the intelligentsia supported women and girls learning—so long as they were tutored privately, at home, as was proper. But Yuan, a famous poet known as a ladies' man and all-around scamp, was having them come to *his* house. He even published a book of poems by his lady students.

By now, Yuan's devout, religious friends had probably given up on saving him. He had always said he found the study of sutras boring ("…alas, before I had finished a chapter, I found myself yawning and stretching, and thinking of bed" [Waley, 80].) His especially pious friend Peng Shaosheng 彭紹升 (1740–1796) begged him to reconsider: "Surely," he wrote, "where we came from when we were born and where we shall go when we die are questions of the utmost importance, and cannot be simply ignored." Yuan Mei wrote back, "I think they can" (Waley, 81).

On this subject, he remained obstinate up to the moment he wrote his will:

As for recitation of Scriptures, chanting liturgies and entertainment of monks on the seventh days—these are things I have always detested. You may tell your sisters to come and make an offering to me, in which case I shall certainly accept it; or to come once and wail; at which I shall be deeply moved. But if monks come to the door, at the first sound of their wooden clappers, my divine soul will stop up its ears and run away, which I am sure you would not like. (Waley, 202)

He also asked his heirs to keep the house and garden the same, with everything intact as it was in his lifetime. "If that can be kept up for thirty years, I shall rest contented in my grave. Of any longer period it is useless to think" (Waley, 200). His descendants actually preserved everything in place until 1853, when the property was destroyed during the Taiping Rebellion (1850–1864). The Sui Garden is now a symbol, a memory, and over two hundred years later, nowhere is the place more vividly recalled than in the world of Chinese food. Chinese chefs today still proudly present dishes from this book, which is a tribute to the enduring and prismatic depth of Yuan's contribution: he saw perfected cuisine not just as the ultimate attainment of sensory pleasure, but as art, as philosophy, and as a matter of principle.

Before he died, he ordered his tomb inscribed with these words: "Tomb of Yuan, of the Sui Yuan, Qing Dynasty. For a thousand autumns and ten thousand generations, there will certainly be those who will appreciate me" (Waley, 201).

I am one. And now you will be, too.

Translator's Note

By *Sean J. S. Chen*

I first read about *The Way of Eating* (also known as *Recipes from the Garden of Contentment*, a more literal translation of the Chinese title *Suiyuan Shidan* 隨園食單) in 2013, when I became interested in the history of Chinese cuisine. I immediately noticed experts and enthusiasts alike pointing to this book as essential reading in the study and understanding of modern Chinese gastronomy. Some authors even provided snippets of translations and recipes. Alas, after searching online for several weeks, I was left disappointed: there were no full English translations of the book and only incomplete or unsourced modern Chinese translations.

There was, of course, the original, written in Classical Chinese during the late eighteenth century. Classical Chinese is a written language of its own, quite different from modern written Chinese. For the untrained reader, Classical Chinese appears as a discontinuous mass of characters glommed together on a grid without any punctuation to guide the reader.

Reading through the Classical Chinese brought back those feelings of inadequacy I felt while grinding through the Middle English version of the *Canterbury Tales* in university. Still, without any English translation to work from and wanting very much to try the "ancient" recipes and heed the gastronomic advice doled out by Yuan Mei, I had no other choice but to delve head-on into the Classical Chinese text.

One night I sat down and started taking notes, looking up phrases, noting sources, and writing about the things that interested me along the way. After several days, I completed my first translation of the section on bird's nest. Rereading that first version now, it certainly has its share of rough spots and errors, but at the time, the ego boost from this success motivated me to translate another section a few days later. And then another. This went on for about a month or two, then I started to notice a change. What started out as a slow grind through opaque blocks of Classical Chinese started taking less effort, and I found that I could read and understand more and more without trouble. I decided that I might as well continue—posting my translations on a blog once a week as motivation— and see where it took me.

Some Chinese scholars thought well enough of the translations on my blog to mention them to Karen Christensen of Berkshire Publishing Group. She approached me in 2015 about publishing the full translated work as a book. At that time, I was barely more than halfway done with the translation of the text. Needless to say, the pace of the project picked up rapidly. Soon I was translating several sections a week, while commuting to and from work, late in the evenings after work, and on weekends alongside to family responsibilities.

The scope and requirements of the project also grew beyond that of the original website. Not only was the glossary expanded, and annotations refined, but the translation was also reworked after feedback from E. N. (Gene) Anderson and Jeffrey Riegel.

These China scholars were enthusiastic about how I, as someone coming from a background in the sciences rather than the field of Chinese studies, was approaching the translation. Nevertheless, being outside the field, I required advice and guidance only experts can provide. In particular, Gene made detailed suggestions and was especially adamant on the subject of translating the original text as literally as possible in order to show readers Yuan Mei's specific literary style and humor. For example, rather than translating a phrase like *fen wei bing tan* 分為冰炭 with English clichés such as "as different as night and day" or simply as "different," Gene recommended sticking to the literal meaning of "as different as ice and coal." Eventually, I translated the phrase as "as different as burning embers and ice."

The first two chapters of the book ("Essential Knowledge" and "Objectionables") can be thought of as the "theory" chapters, where Yuan Mei decrees the dos and don'ts of Chinese cuisine. I find these chapters most interesting and rewarding, because they provide a set of fundamentals that one can use to understand Chinese cuisine and gastronomy. In fact, we could go so far as to say that they codify the more important parts of the cuisine's traditional aesthetics and principles. It also bears noting that many of the rules and specifications in these two chapters can be applied to other cuisines without much modification, which may itself hint at the existence of some universal truths in gastronomy.

The remaining chapters in the book are made up primarily of recipes and dishes that Yuan Mei found significant enough to mention after years of eating the good foods that eighteenth-century Chinese cuisine had to offer. Within these recipes, he also included a bit of cooking theory specific to the ingredients, as well as stories about the people and events that paint a picture of his life. These short sketches punctuate the monotony of page after page of ingredients and cooking techniques and makes for rather interesting, if not insightful, reading.

One must keep in mind that like most Chinese literati, Yuan Mei rarely if ever entered the kitchen himself and probably did not have any appreciable cooking skills. These old recipes should be considered as rough and somewhat distorted images filtered through the eyes of Yuan Mei, which would inevitably produce rather poor or inedible dishes if followed without interpolation and interpretation. Even Yuan Mei himself openly admitted this in the preface, stating, "Static written recipes cannot match the full expression of a living chef" and that "there is no need to exert oneself in trying to distill complete bodies of knowledge from old yellowing texts." In the end, one must concede when reading any old book on gastronomy, be it by Yuan Mei, Apicius, or Brillat-Savarin, that any dish now existing only as a written recipe has more or less died with the chef who knew how to make it. What remains are arguably just artifacts that bear witness to the dishes' historical existence.

I spent a large amount of time and effort on the identification of ingredients. While most ingredients have had consistent names since the eighteenth century in Zhejiang Province, China, and the surrounding regions, there are still enough differences that made this task very challenging at times. For instance, pinpointing the "yellow fish" (*huangyu*) as the yellow croaker required research into Chinese fishery and trade at the time, understanding the migratory and reproductive habits of several candidate fish, and knowing the Chinese historical and taxonomy names.

The identification of cooking techniques and their parameters has also proven difficult. Specifically, the lack of historical resources on the details of the techniques requires us to go the more "experimental archeology" route, where translations are based loosely on our own experiences of re-creating the dishes, looking into the food sciences literature, or referring to modern Chinese recipes using similar techniques. An example of this would be the process of figuring out the approximate length of time represented by the unit *gun* 滚, where we provided an educated guess (namely three seconds) by calibrating it to the expected cooking times of the ingredients mentioned.

There is much joy to be had in trying to reconstruct these dishes. In China, there are restaurants, cookbooks, and chefs that specialize in Yuan Mei's dishes. For those outside of the Chinese culinary tradition, success might be easier to achieve if one begins with recipes that are relatively simple, have modern-day analogues, or provide sufficient details on preparation. I recommend the following to the adventurous reader.

Fake foods (jia 假):

- Imitation Crab (p. 51)
- Imitation Milk (p. 84)
- Imitation Pheasant Rolls (p. 93)
- Imitation Shad (in "White Amur Bream") (p. 108)

Home-style foods (jia chang 家常):

- *Luosuo* Pork (and the Three Pork Dishes from Duanzhou) (p. 74)
- Home-Style Pan-Fried Fish (p. 113)
- Taro Braised with Bok Choy (p. 142)

*Comfort food, or food for senior citizens (yi yu lao ren*宜於老人):

- Chicken Congee (p. 89)
- Chicken Blood (p. 96)
- Sesame Greens (p. 152)

I am extremely grateful to Diane, Celine, and Alex for putting up with my mess, physical and otherwise. Special thanks goes to my parents for forcing me to learn to read and write Chinese. Many spiral notebooks were mutilated for the cause.

About Sean Jy-Shyang Chen

Sean Jy-Shyang Chen is a research scientist and algorithms developer for computer-assisted minimally invasive neurosurgery. He is the founder and former director of a company specializing in medical calibration devices and image processing. This is his first publication outside the field of science and engineering. His adventures of translating can also be found on his blog, *The Way of the Eating* (https://wayoftheeating.wordpress.com).

A Note on Measurements

By the time Yuan Mei wrote *The Way of Eating*, measurements in China were largely standardized. Depending on the product being measured, however, the actual amount could still differ. For example, a Chinese ounce (*liang*) of rice may have been more than an ounce of sugar. Similarly, measurements could vary by location, meaning that Yuan Mei's spoon or scoop (*shao*) may have been different from that of his contemporaries in northern or western China. In addition, nonstandard measurements, like a wine cup to measure volume or an incense stick to measure time, are even harder to define. Below are the estimated modern conversions for the measurements that Yuan Mei uses in his recipes. The official units are based on those utilized during the Qing dynasty. Detailed explanations for the amounts of a cup, a wine cup, a *gun* ("moment"), and an incense stick can be found in the glossary.

Chinese	Western Equivalent	Modern Measurements (Metric and Imperial)
Volume		
勺 shao	spoon, scoop	10 ml (0.34 fl oz)
合 ge		100 ml (3.4 fl oz)
升 sheng	peck, quart	1,035 L (34 fl oz)
斗 dou	pint	10 L (2 US gal)
杯 bei	cup	around 100 ml (3.4 fl oz)
酒杯 jiubei	wine cup	30 to 50 ml (1 to 1.5 fl oz)
Weight		
錢 qian	mace	3.7 g
兩 liang	teal, Chinese ounce	37 g
斤 jin	catty, Chinese pound	596 g (20.9 oz) a modern-day jin equals 500 g
Length		
分 fen		3 mm (0.12 in)
寸 cun	inch	3.2 cm (1.26 in)
尺 chi	foot	32 cm (12.5 in)
丈 zhang		3.2 m (10.5 ft)
Time		
滾 gun	boil, roll	3 seconds
刻 ke	quarter	15 minutes
香 xiang	incense stick	1 hour
時辰 shichen		2 hours

Source: Endymion Wilkinson. (2010). *Chinese History: A Manual* (pp. 234–246, section 7.3: Weights and Measures).

A Note on Alcohol (*Jiu* 酒)

The Chinese word *jiu* 酒 (pronounced "joe" or "jee-oh") describes a wide range of alcoholic beverages. Traditional Chinese brewed or distilled *jiu* is produced using a unique fermentation process. The grains (typically rice) are first cooked and then inoculated with a grain-based starter known as *qu* 麴. Different types of starters are used for different alcoholic drinks and suited to different climates. All starters, however, are made of grain (or grain flour) colonized by special fungi. These fungi, typically from the genus *Aspergillus* or *Rhizopus*, secrete the enzyme amylase that breaks down the grains' large starch molecules into simple sugars. The sugar is then converted to alcohol by the strains of yeast in the starter. These fungi and yeast also produce large amounts of aldehydes and other fragrance compounds that give traditional *jiu* its aroma.

The process of making *jiu* typically begins by pulverizing blocks of the starter, mixing it with the cooked grains, such as rice or sorghum, and then allowing this mixture to ferment and liquefy into a semisolid fermented mash. If brewed *jiu* is the final product, then the mash is transferred into fine-meshed cotton bags and pressed to separate the alcoholic beverage from the sticky grain fibers. Distilled *jiu* is processed somewhat differently: the mash is usually drier and is directly steam-distilled without pressing, in the same manner as French marc or Italian grappa.

Considering these unique production techniques, finding an accurate English translation for *jiu* that also preserves the word's cultural context is difficult. Most works on Chinese cuisine or culture, past or modern, typically translate *jiu* as "wine," "rice wine," "rice spirits," or "Chinese liquor." These, however, are poor choices. Western wines are almost always made from fruit juices naturally high in simple sugar content (disaccharides or monosaccharides), and the term "wine" would thus account only for brewed *jiu*. "Liquor" or "spirit," while decent terms for referring to distilled *jiu*, leave out all other alcoholic drinks that *jiu* represents.

Some translators have suggested that *jiu* should be translated as "beer," since that technically refers to alcoholic drinks brewed from grains (or cereals). While this translation may be compelling at first glance, on further examination, it also falls short. First, it ignores the fact that Western beers are usually made with malted barley instead of fungi to saccharify (i.e., turn starch into sugar) grain starch, which drastically changes the drink's flavor. Thus, brewed *jiu* would likely never be recognized by a connoisseur as "beer." If we were to extend the logic for calling brewed *jiu* "beer," then distilled *jiu* would technically be called "whiskey," which would be just as unsuitable due to their differences in flavor. Second, many *jiu* have excellent aging potential, like that of Western wines and distilled liquors, which cannot be said for most (Western) beers. Last, and perhaps most importantly, the cultural connotation of traditional *jiu* is much more similar to that of wines and liquors in the West, which are used for toasting in formal celebratory events and consumed for creative inspiration or drowning sorrows.

In short, none of the existing translations for *jiu* are really satisfactory. We have made the (perhaps controversial) decision not to try and find a translation that provides both cultural context and technical accuracy—a near to impossible task, as shown above—and instead use the Mandarin pinyin transliteration *jiu* as is. While this may initially feel odd for readers unfamiliar with the Chinese language, we believe that with repetition, the discomfort of this "foreign" word will quickly fade, and it will gain the familiarity of other adopted foreign words, like kimchi, sushi, Camembert, or ketchup. While most mentions of *jiu* 酒 in the Chinese texts have been transliterated as such, an exception has been made for instances where the term occurs in combination with other words, for example, "wine cup" and "wine lees."

For those readers interested in the details of making *jiu*, Y. H. Hui's *Handbook of Food Science, Technology, and Engineering* (2005, volume 4) and Joseph Needham's well-known *Science and Civilization in China* (volume 6) provide valuable information.

PREFACE

Although matters of food and drink can be considered somewhat trivial, I have earnestly said all that I wish to say from my heart, and for that I regret nothing!

Poets of the past praised the Duke of Zhou by saying, "His table-ware was arranged in a straight and orderly fashion," and they criticized Fan Bo by saying, "Coarse grains of the past, delicate grains of the present."[1] From this, we can see how cuisine was something of great importance even to the ancients.

Indeed, matters pertaining to cuisines are well represented in the ancient Confucian Classics. The *Classic of Changes* touched upon cooking techniques, the *Classic of Documents* touched upon flavoring food and seasonings, and brief discussions on matters of cuisine are scattered throughout the section "The Village" in the *Analects of Confucius* and the chapter "The Pattern of the Family" in the *Classic of Rites*. Even the philosopher Mencius, who considered cuisine something frivolous, nevertheless expressed that it is not possible to savor one's food and drink properly in abject hunger and thirst. It is clear that trying to cover such a broad subject as cuisine will not be an easy feat.

In the *Doctrine of the Mean*, it also says, "Everybody eats and drinks, but those who can understand and discern the flavors are few and far between." In the *Discourse on Literature*,[2] it is said, "It takes an elder a lifetime to understand how to lodge and live, but it would take him three lifetimes to fully understand how to eat." The ancients always meticulously prepared food offerings for the rites and ceremonies in accordance with the canon, and were never negligent when performing their duties. It is said that when Confucius was touched by someone's singing, he would ask them to repeat their song and then try to accompany it with his own voice. By this method, he showed how one can improve oneself and acquire new skills from others. I admire this drive to continually improve, and I seek to emulate it at all times. Thus, whenever I have eaten well and been inspired by a meal I have had at someone else's place, I would later send my chef to them to write

---

1 The Duke of Zhou 周公 was a member of the royal family and a major figure during the early years of the Zhou dynasty (1045–256 BCE). Here, the orderly tableware is used to describe his methodical and effective approach to governing the country. At the same time, the ancient poets mentioned coarse grains to allude to a time when rulers were frugal and rugged, and in doing so criticized the minister Fan Bo 凡伯 for being the exact opposite: indulgent and ostentatious, like a serving of delicate grains.

2 *Discourse on Literature* (Dianlun 典論) is a treatise attributed to Cao Pi 曹丕, the son of the Warring States general Cao Cao 曹操.

down the recipes for the dishes and the techniques used in their preparation.

In this manner, over the last forty years, I have managed to compile and assemble recipes for many delectable dishes. Some of the techniques and recipes for the dishes are recorded in their entirety, some are around 60 to 70 percent complete, some have only been recorded in fragments that are 20 or 30 percent complete, while others can only be described superficially or by a title. I have sincerely asked each household for their recipes to gather them here. Thus, even though some of the recipes and techniques are not fully detailed, I have nevertheless been able to note the dishes' flavors and the houses they came from, as a show of gratitude for their generosity and for the sake of posterity. Such is the nature of one with an inquisitive mind.

Of course, static written recipes cannot match the full expression of a living chef, just as even the most capable writer cannot produce a flawless work.[3] As such, there is no need to exert oneself in trying to distill complete bodies of knowledge from old yellowing texts. If someone says, "Everybody has their own preferences, just as they all have different faces, how can you be so sure that their tastes will match your own in any way?" To that I say, "Like arranging a marriage and chopping wood for an axe handle, if things are done in an orderly and practical manner, then the results will not be too far off the mark."[4] I cannot guarantee that all the people under heaven will have the same tastes as I do, but I can still introduce them to dishes and recipes that I fancy.

---

3 The idea conveyed here is that even the best recipe will never replace the full abilities of a chef, just as writers are unable to reflect the full dimensions and complexity of the subjects they are describing.

4 This is a reference to the poem "Making Axe Handles" 伐柯 from the *Classic of Poetry* 詩經:

How does one hew an axe handle?
　It is not possible without an axe.
How does one get a wife?
　It is not possible without a matchmaker.
Oh hewing axe handles, hewing axe handles,
　the product isn't too far off the mark.
And when I see the right woman [for marriage],
　all the tableware will be lined up in a row.

The last line of the poem is also quoted in the first sentence of the preface, creating a circular reference to the Duke of Zhou's tableware.

Although matters of food and drink can be considered somewhat trivial, I have earnestly said all that I wish to say from my heart, and for that I regret nothing!

As for the book *The Domain of Texts*,[5] which lists thirty types of food and drink, as well as the works of the calligrapher and painter Mei Gong and author and playwright Li Weng, I have personally tested all their recipes. This has resulted, however, in nothing but offensive and noxious dishes. I conclude that, for the most part, these works are the results of the overextended imaginations of mediocre scholars, and as such I have cited nothing from them.[6]

---

5 *The Domain of Texts* (*Shuofu* 說郛, sometimes translated as *Environs of Fiction*) is a fourteenth-century encyclopedic work by Tao Zongyi 陶宗儀 (c. 1320–c. 1402).

6 During his days as an imperial officer, colleagues of Yuan Mei told him that his sharp tongue left a trail of devastation behind him. This is an example of that; clearly age did not dull it.

Dos and Don'ts of Chinese Cuisines

In the following two chapters, "Essential Knowledge" and "Objectionables," Yuan Mei presents a set of "ground rules" for cooking Chinese dishes. This theoretical foundation shines a light on what makes Chinese cuisine unique. Yuan Mei frequently refers to classical works from the Chinese canon such as Confucius's *Analects*, and *The Classic of Rites*, and incorporates typical Chinese philosophical ideas such as the Way and the theory of Five Flavors.

These basics also show how Yuan Mei's approach to food was surprisingly modern and universal. For example, he believes in bringing out natural flavors and seasonality, controlling or diffusing stronger flavors and odors, and even considers issues of animal rights. In the section on color and fragrance, Yuan Mei observes that we experience and identify food not only through our sense of taste, but also through sight and smell, and he denounces the practice of using caramelized sugar or fragrance compounds to enhance the color or smell of a dish—common in today's food industry.

It is clear here, as in the Preface, that Yuan Mei was not afraid to express his likes and dislikes about techniques, skills, dishes, chefs, and intellectuals of his time. For example, he repeatedly dismisses the gastronomic tastes and customs of the people from Jinling (modern-day Nanjing).

Yuan Mei also happily scolds diners for getting drunk before or during a meal and hosts for pushing their personal tastes on their guests, as well as chefs whose efforts fail to impress him. In general, the literati did not have a very high opinion of their chefs. This can be seen through the classical Chinese concept of *san jiao jiu liu* 三教九流, in which the three traditional belief systems and nine traditional professions were classified and ranked in a manner similar to a caste system. Rulers and officials ranked at the top, of course, while merchants and workers ended up near the bottom. Needless to say, chefs did not fare well in these rankings. In an even more fine-grained social "worthiness" classification (*shehui jiuliu* 社會九流) people were split and ranked into twenty-seven different occupations, with chefs relegated to near the very bottom. That said, Yuan Mei himself was very fond of his own chefs, most notably Wang Xiaoyu, for whom he wrote an emotional obituary.

Essential Knowledge

In the scholarly arts, one must first understand something before putting it into practice. It is the same with the culinary arts. Assembled here is the list of essential knowledge.

Basic Nature

All things have their basic nature, just as everybody has their own qualities. If a person is by nature dim-witted, any attempts to school him would be pointless, even if it were Confucius or Mencius doing the teaching. Similarly, if one uses ingredients of low quality, even the extraordinary culinary skills of the famous chef Yi Ya would produce something mediocre. The following is a broad overview on choosing ingredients: Good pork should have thin skin and lack any strong or foul smells. Good chicken should be tender, and neither too old and tough nor too young and underdeveloped. Good quality crucian carp should have flat bodies with white bellies; carp with dark backs are less suitable for eating. Eels fished from the lakes and streams are exquisite, while those that have lived in the large rivers tend to be scrawny and full of spines and bone. Grain-fed ducks should be round and fat such that their flesh is pale. Soil-mounded bamboo shoots with fewer segments taste fresher and sweeter.

The technique of mounding soil on top of growing shoots to keep them white is known as "blanching," a term that is also used to describe a rather different process of immersing food quickly in boiling water. In the West, the process is usually used for growing white asparagus and prevents them from acquiring a slightly bitter flavor and becoming tough, as it does for the bamboo shoots here.

The differences between the quality of a good ham and a bad one are as far apart as sea and sky. As for the salted fish of Taizhou, the differences are like burning embers and ice. The same sort of reasoning applies to other foodstuffs. For the quality of a banquet's dishes, 60 percent of the credit goes to the chef, but the remaining 40 percent goes to the person who selected the ingredients.

Dried salted fish (*xiang* 鲞) is typically made from yellow croaker.

Condiments

The condiments used by a chef for seasoning are like the clothing and jewelry on a woman. A beautiful woman, when garbed in ragged and worn clothing, looks unattractive. Even the renowned

|Spring and Autumn Period beauty| Xi Shi cannot look beautiful under such conditions.

When someone well versed in cuisine chooses soy sauce, they will buy only that which was made in the heat of summer and, prior to using it, will taste it for sweetness. When they flavor dishes with oil, they will use sesame oil, checking whether it has been roasted or is still raw. When seasoning with *jiu*, they will use one that has been freshly filtered from the fermenting mash. When seasoning with vinegar, they will use rice vinegar, demanding a product with high clarity. One must also understand that soy sauce has its light and dark varieties, oils may come from animal or plant sources, *jiu* have sweet and dry varieties, and vinegars may either be young or aged. One must make these distinctions and not be careless in the choice of seasonings. Other condiments such as green onions, Sichuan pepper, ginger, cinnamon, sugar, and salt are used in lesser quantities. Even then, one should choose only the best that one can get. Note, too, that autumn sauce sold in Suzhou is available in different grades: high, medium, and low. Finally, although Zhenjiang vinegar has excellent color, its taste is so mild that it has lost its essence as vinegar. In this regard, the vinegar of Banpu is the best, with that from Pukou in second place.

> The term *jiu* 酒 is often translated as wine, but actually describes a wide range of alcoholic beverages. Rather than translating, it will be referred to as *jiu* throughout this text. For a detailed discussion of the term, see page xxvi.

> Autumn sauce (*qiuyou* 秋油, lit. autumn oil) is a high-quality soy sauce, pressed in late autumn, hence its name.

Cleaning

The requirements of cleaning and washing specific ingredients are as follows: One must remove all feathers from bird's nests, remove all mud from within sea cucumbers, remove all sand from shark's fins, and eliminate the foul smells from deer tendon. If the meat contains sinews, one needs to remove them so that the meat can remain tender after cooking. Duck kidneys have a foul odor, therefore, be sure to remove them and rinse the cavity well. Be careful not to break the fish's gallbladder when gutting and cleaning the fish, because doing so will render the entire dish bitter. If one does not wash away the

The "white tendon" is not actually a tendon but a long mucus-filled structure, known as the lateral line canal, located just underneath the skin on the lateral line (a series of organs to detect pressure and vibration) of the fish. Known in modern Chinese as a "fishy-smelling tendon or thread" (*xingjin* 腥筋 or *xingxian* 腥線), this canal is paired with the lateral line nerve, and together they help the fish sense subtle pressure changes in the water. In some fish species, it is used to sense the electrical potentials from the muscles of their prey. The mucus in this canal likely acquires the smell of mud and water, and spoils when the fish dies, which necessitates its removal to prevent spreading the smell to the rest of the fish during cooking. This removal is particularly important for freshwater fish, and especially for carp.

slime of an eel during its preparation, the resulting dish will have an unpleasant fishy odor. One must remove any old leaves when cleaning garlic chives, leaving only the tender white stems. When preparing leaf vegetables, one should remove the coarser outside leaves and use only the heart. In the chapter "The Patterns of the Family" in the *Classic of Rites*, it is said, "One should remove the orbital bones around a fish's eyes and remove the *orifices* of the soft-shell turtle," admonishing us to diligently clean all ingredients in a dish. The proverb "If you want a fish to taste good, wash it until the white tendons come out" also highlights the truth behind these facts.

Seasoning

When seasoning a dish, one must take the character of a dish's ingredients into consideration. Some ingredients require both *jiu* and water in seasoning, some use only *jiu*, while others use only water. Some ingredients use both salt and soy sauce, some use only light soy sauce, while others use only salt. Some ingredients are rich-flavored and greasy, which requires a thorough pan-frying with oil before further preparation.[1] Some ingredients smell raw or fishy, which requires treatment with a drizzle of vinegar. Some ingredients need seasoning with sugar to enhance their savory sweetness. Yet other ingredients benefit greatly from some drying.

---

1 An example of this is Dongpo pork (*Dongpo rou* 東坡肉), in which the pork belly is first boiled and then pan-fried on each side. The skin side should be a toasted, golden-brown color. This creates a rather fatty pork dish that is "rich but not greasy" (*fei er bu ni* 肥而不膩).

This is especially true in pan-fried or stir-fried dishes since it allows surrounding seasonings and flavors to better permeate the dish's ingredients.[2] There are also ingredients that exhibit their best when cooked in a soup, since this allows their exquisite flavors to meld and contribute to the broth. Examples of this are the swimming and floating aquatic ingredients.

Accompaniment

It is said in a proverb, "For each type of woman there is a matching man." In the *Classic of Rites* it is said, "Compare a person with those most similar to him." Are the methods of cuisine any different?

The success of a dish depends on its ingredients' mutual support and accompaniment. One should accompany light-tasting ingredients with other light-tasting ingredients, rich ingredients with other rich ingredients, soft ingredients with the soft, and firm ingredients with the firm. This way they are well matched and in harmony. Note that some ingredients, such as mushrooms, fresh bamboo shoots, and winter melon, can be used as accompaniment in either meat or vegetarian dishes. Ingredients that accompany rich meat dishes well but not vegetable dishes include green onions, garlic chives, fennel seeds, and garlic. Ingredients that accompany vegetable dishes well but not meat dishes include celery, lily bulbs, and sword beans (*Canavalia gladiate*).

I often see crab roe being added into bird's nest soup and lily bulbs being cooked with chicken and pork. This is like having two men of opposite character facing each other, such as the mythic sage emperor Tang Yao and the Jin dynasty general Su Jun—a completely ridiculous act. That said, there are ingredients that coordinate well despite being on opposite sides. For instance, one can quite effectively use vegetable oil to stir-fry meats and use animal fat to stir-fry vegetable items.

---

2 This suggestion may be related to the process of slightly salting tofu and patting it dry prior to pan-frying. This draws out moisture from the surface of the otherwise soft tofu and allows it to take on a slightly crisp pellicle when pan-fried. To make this dish, all one needs is good tofu, oil, and salt. Drizzle in some good soy sauce, and you get a simple yet delectable and satisfying dish. Drying the outside of food before pan-frying is also often done in Western cuisine with steak and chops to promote flavorful Maillard reactions.

Lone Ingredients

Ingredients with strong flavors are best when used on their own without accompaniment, much in the way the likes of chancellor Li Jiang and minister Zhang Juzheng must be allowed to work on their own to make the best use of their talents. For instance, eel, soft-shell turtle, crab, abalone, beef, and lamb are ingredients best used in dishes on their own without another main ingredient. Why? The above ingredients have rich flavors that are thick and assertive. As such, their flaws are quite apparent and thus require the seasoning and harmonization provided by the five flavors to control them. This allows these ingredients to show off their strength while hiding their deficiencies.

The Chinese five flavors are:
- pungent (*xin* 辛)
- salty (*xian* 咸)
- sour (*suan* 酸)
- bitter (*ku* 苦)
- sweet (*gan* 甘)

They correspond to the five Daoist elements metal, water, wood, fire, and earth. This insistence on having only five "canonical" flavors more or less resulted in the neglected exploration of umami/savory (*xian* 鲜) and fat (*you* 油) flavors, even though they have been known for hundreds of years.

So who would willingly abandon these principles and even go the extra step to push things beyond good taste? Well, leave it to the people in Jinling [modern-day Nanjing], who enjoy combining sea cucumbers with turtle, and shark's fin with crab meat. When I see this pairing of ingredients, I cannot help but frown with displeasure. I feel that in these combinations, the flavor of turtle and crab is diluted and made bland by the sea cucumber and shark's fin, while the unpleasant flavors of the sea cucumber and shark's fin harm the turtle and crab, and contaminate their tastes, all to the dish's detriment.

Heat Control

In the art of cooking, the most important skill is one's ability to control heat. Some ingredients require a fierce flame, such as those being pan-fried or stir-fried. If a gentle flame is used on such ingredients, they will become wilted and lifeless. Some ingredients require a gentle flame, such as those for stewing, since using

"Heat control" (*huo hou* 火候) describes the process of controlling both the intensity of the cooking heat and the length of time that the food is in contact with the heat. "Flame control" would be an alternative translation, since Chinese cooking without a real flame can be considered slightly impaired, *even* with new induction technologies. This section uses the terms *wu huo* 武火 and *wen huo* 文火 to describe very high cooking heat and low cooking heat, respectively. In this context, *wu* and *wen* can be interpreted as "fierce" and "gentle," but these terms also commonly refer to "warlike" or "martial" and "cultured" or "civil." "Martial flames" and "cultured flames" are idioms clearly illustrating the kind of relationship and interactions a Chinese chef has with this element. One contemporary chef even stated that every dish he made was "negotiated from the flames." In respect to Yuan Mei describing the force of a flame with *wen* and *wu*, we see it cast as an elemental spirit with which the chef must seek partnership, sparring with its chaotic martial sides and conversing with its calm cultured sides to produce a perfectly prepared dish.

an aggressive flame will make such ingredients tough and dry. Others ingredients require cooking in the beginning with a fierce flame and finishing with a gentle flame, such as those dishes with ingredients requiring sauce reductions. If one is impatient during the reduction process and uses heat that is too strong, the ingredient's surface will be charred while the inside remains raw. Certain ingredients become tender with prolonged cooking, such as kidneys and chicken eggs; however, some ingredients, such as fresh fish and clams, will not become tender even if exposed to a slightly stronger flame. When one does not remove meat from the heat in a timely manner after its completion, its color will not be an appetizing red but rather a charred black. Likewise, a fish not removed from the heat in a timely manner will not be tender and "alive," but rather dry, overcooked, and "dead." If you frequently open the pot's lid while the food is cooking, it will have foamy sauces and be less fragrant. As well, if you attempt to relight a spent flame while cooking, the ingredients will be rendered of their oil[3] and become flavorless.

The Daoists attain perfection of sainthood by channeling their internal forces through "nine revolutions," and the Confucians

---

3 The idea here is that if you are cooking over a twig- or straw-fired flame, and it goes out while the meat is still being cooked, restarting the flame would produce low heat, causing the meat to stew and render its fat.

attain perfection by learning from their errors and striving to over-come failure.[4] Likewise, if chefs know how to control the flame and attend to it diligently and attentively, they, too, are close to attain-ing the Way. When eating fish, if the flesh is as translucent white as jade and holds together without flaking apart, this is tender and "live" flesh. But if the flesh is white, opaque as powdered starch, and falling apart, this is "dead" flesh. To have a fresh fish and then cook it until it is stale and flavorless is something truly despicable.

Color and Fragrance

As neighbors of the mouth, the eyes and the nose act as guides while eating. When a dish is seen and smelled, its color and fra-grance is compounded. If the dish looks crisp and clear as the autumn clouds, its color as voluptuous as amber, and its alluring fragrance wafts into the nose, one does not need to feel a piece of the food against one's teeth or taste it with one's tongue to know how delicious it actually is. It should be noted, however, that in wanting color in a dish, one should not resort to using caramel-ized sugar. In wanting fragrance, one should not resort to using flavorants. Once such "makeup" is applied, a dish's true flavors are obscured and irreparably damaged.

Speed

When inviting guests, one normally sets the event three days in advance so that there is enough time to put together a well-con-certed and varied menu. But if there are unplanned guests and food needs to be served quickly, or guests arrive unannounced outside the door or drop in by boat, how does one take the waters

---

4 The internal forces (*dan* 丹) are a Daoist concept of the fluid or elixir manifestation of qi-like forces (*danqi* 丹氣) in one's body. The Daoist "nine revolutions" are tiers of transformation needed to imbue the body or a different substance with mystical powers. The concepts of "not committing errors" (*wuguo* 無過) and "believing in inadequacy" (*buji* 不及) are important guides to the conduct of a Confucian *junzi* (true gentlemen). The former concept is well summed up in the *Zuo Commentary on the Spring and Autumn Annals* (*Chunqiu Zuozhuan* 春秋左傳:宣公二年), which says, "Who among us has not erred? To err and be able to correct oneself, there is nothing better than this". The latter is well understood through a quote from the *Analects of Confucius*: "Study diligently as if you're about to fail and as if you're about to be surpassed".

Lees are the solids left over from the production of rice wine after the wine has been pressed out of the fermented mass, which consists of yeast, aspergillus, and loose fiber from the endosperm of the milled rice grains. Due to the fiber, rice wine lees are quite different from the lees of Western beers and wines, which consist primarily of yeast. Rice wine lees are more similar to the leftover marc from pressed red wine must (the pulp and skins of crushed grapes) with its high fiber content, than to the sticky, pasty lees that settles from rosé and some white wine production.

Fish pickled in rice wine lees is quite popular in Shandong Province. In fact, pickling food in lees is a well-known and loved flavoring and preservation method in all centers of rice-wine production in China and East Asia. For instance, Japan is well-known for its *kasuzuke* (fish or vegetables pickled in sake lees) and *narazuke* (fruit or vegetables pickled in sake and mirin lees).

---

of the Eastern Sea to put out the raging flames at the Western Pond?[5] In these cases, one needs to have a set of quick-to-prepare dishes, such as stir-fried chicken slices, pork strips, and dried shrimp with tofu, or the likes of fish pickled in rice wine lees, and tea-smoked ham.[6] These versatile dishes can be quickly prepared on short notice. One cannot be ignorant of them.

Transformations

Each ingredient has its own unique character and cannot be mixed without confusing its flavor. As Confucius said, "Students must each be taught according to their aptitude and not just according to one standard." Such is the way to elevate oneself to become a true gentlemen.

These days we see flamboyant chefs boiling chickens, ducks, pigs, and geese together in soup, producing dishes with tastes indistinguishable from, and as flavorful as, chewing on wax. I fear the souls of the chickens, pigs, geese, and ducks seeing such wrongs done will be demanding justice from the courts in the afterlife. A competent chef would prepare the right cooking vessels and

---

5 This is a proverb describing a predicament where one must resolve a situation with minimal resources at hand.

6 This is a dry-cured smoked ham from Yunnan Province.

utensils; such that each ingredient can offer its best and each dish can show off its flavors to the fullest. This way, when connoisseurs taste the food, they will be inexplicably and thoroughly delighted by the flavors, as if a flower has blossomed in their hearts.

Tableware

The ancients said, "Good food cannot match good tableware," indicating the importance in choosing one's bowls and dishes. Tableware from the reigns of emperors Xuande, Chenghua, Jiajing, and Wanli,[7] however, is so precious that it leaves one anxious and nervous about breaking it during use. One would rather use contemporary tableware fired from the imperial kilns, which is at once refined and beautiful. Note that foods more suited for bowls should be served in bowls, food suited for plates served on plates, large foods served in larger tableware, and smaller foods served in smaller tableware. Thus, even when there are gross shortcomings in a banquet, the table's setting would still feel coordinated and delightful. If one blindly insists on adhering to the traditional

---

"Ten bowls and eight dishes" is a name for a traditional celebratory banquet that also defines what should be included, namely ten large bowls for main dishes and eight small plates for side dishes. Similarly, the phrase *sancai yitang* 三菜一湯 describes a meal of three main dishes and a soup but is also used to denote a standard Chinese family meal. In this case, Yuan Mei decries those who follow these phrases literally, since a celebratory meal should contain as many dishes as the guests and host desire. This describes a traditional banquet with ten big bowls for main dishes and eight smaller plates for the side dishes. Yuan Mei decries those who follow the phrase literally, rather than serving as many dishes as the host and guests desire, with attention to the right tableware and table setting. The related phrase *san cai yi tang* 三菜一湯 means a meal consisting of three main dishes (*sancai*) and one soup (*yi tang*), also used to describe a standard Chinese family meal.

---

7 In dynastic times, the reign name of an emperor used to denote a historical period. Xuande, Chenghua, Jiajing, and Wanli were emperors during the Ming dynasty. The tableware from these periods was highly valued during Yuan Mei's time in the subsequent Qing dynasty.

"ten bowls and eight dishes" in a banquet, instead of considering how best to serve the food, others might suspect one of being dull-witted.

Expensive food items should typically be served in larger tableware, while more common foods can be served on small tableware. Pan-fried or stir-fried foods are best served on plates, and soups and stews served in bowls. Pan-fried or stir-fried foods are best prepared in iron woks, while stewed foods are best prepared in clay sand pots.

Table Service

The technique for table service is as follows: salty items should be served before bland items; thick and rich items should be served before thin and light items; dry dishes should be served before soupy dishes. There are five flavors under heaven, so one should not be limited to serving only one. When the guests are getting full, one should serve dishes with spicy and hot flavors to stimulate their appetites. When the guests have drunk too much *jiu* and are fatigued by the alcohol, one should serve sweet and sour foods to reawaken their stomachs.

Seasons

Black pepper is the dried fruit of *Piper nigrum*. Yuan Mei does not specify black or white pepper, though Chinese kitchens traditionally use white peppercorns.

Summer days are long and hot, which causes meat to spoil if the animal is slaughtered too soon. Winter days are short and cold, which causes food to be undercooked if the cooking time is shortened. Beef and lamb are best eaten in the wintertime and are not good for consumption during summer. Cured hams and preserved meats are good for eating during summer but are not as well suited for winter. As for condiments, ground mustard is suited for summer, and pepper for winter.

If one can find preserved winter vegetables in the peak of summer, even a once lowly ingredient becomes a treasure. When one finds tough thin bamboo shoots during autumn, even such a typically worthless food becomes a precious item. Some ingredients are at their best when eaten early during their season, such as Reeves shad (*Tenualosa reevisii*) in March. Some ingredients are best late in their season, such as taro in April. All ingredients are similar in this manner.

Still, some ingredients can no longer be used when they are too old. For instance, when mature, daikon roots become hollow and dry, bamboo shoots become bitter, and Japanese grenadier anchovies (*Coilia nasus*) become bony and hard. Such is the nature of life, where a thing grows and prospers only to fade away, sapped of its strength and vitality.[8]

Quantity

It is better to use more of an expensive ingredient in a dish and less of the inexpensive ones. If too much of an ingredient is pan-fried or stir-fried at a time, there would be insufficient heat to cook them through; meats done this way are especially tough. As such, a cooked meat dish should not have more than half a *jin* of pork and no more than six *liang* of chicken or fish. If one asks, "What if there isn't enough to eat?" I say, "If you're not full after you've finished what's there, just cook some more." Some foods, however, such as white-cooked pork, need to be prepared in large quantities above twenty *jin* in order to taste good, otherwise the resulting dish will be bland and flavorless.[9] Congee also follows this principle; a pot of congee made with less than one *dou* of rice will not be thick enough. Thus, the amount of water needs to be reduced in cooking lesser quantities of congee. Too much water with too little rice would result in a congee that is thin in both texture and flavor.

Jin, *liang*, and *dou* are Qing dynasty measurements. One *jin* equals 590 grams, one *liang* equals 36.9 grams, and one *dou* equals 10 liters.

---

8 One cannot help but wonder if Yuan Mei is being autobiographical here, speaking of his old age and his lower status as a commoner in contrast to a high imperial post in his earlier life.

9 This is true for Eastern and Western stewed items as well. For instance, a small pot of soy-braised pork (*lu rou* 滷肉) or beef stew doesn't have the rich complexity of a larger one.

Cleanliness

Just as a knife used to cut green onions must not be used to cut bamboo shoots, a mortar used to pound peppercorns must not be used to pound flour. A dish that is redolent of a cooking towel indicates that the towel used was not clean, just as a dish that smells like the chopping board means that the board was not clean. It is said in the *Analects of Confucius*, "To do good work, one needs good tools." As such, chefs must be diligent in sharpening their knives, changing their cooking towels, scraping their chopping boards, and washing their hands before preparing food. Even a well-done dish would be inedible if ashes from tobacco, sweat from the chef's brow, flies and ants crawling on the stove, or the soot on the wok were mixed into it. Note, even if it was Xi Shi covered in filth, people would still cover their nose and avoid her.

Using Starch[10]

Bean starch is known as a binder, just as boats are towed using a towline; from each item's name, we can elucidate their use. When someone is shaping ground meat and wishes to make it hold its form, or if they wish to make a soup thick and smooth in texture, they need only to add starch to make it happen. If stir-fried meat sticks to the bottom of the wok, its texture will turn dry. To prevent this, one could simply add some starch to the meat to preserve its texture. Such are the ways of using starch in cooking. When one understands how to use starch, one can make it do wonders in dishes. When people, however, have no idea how to use it, they will make a hilarious mess.

> The Chinese word *qian* 縴, translated here as starch, literally means "velvety and smooth," like silk. This poetic naming alludes to the texture that starch confers to meats and dishes accented with it.

---

10 Any translation of this heading and the word *qian* 縴 in this context would not do it justice. Here it is meant to indicate "starch," but in the most literal sense, it means "velvety and smooth," like silk. This rather poetic naming alludes to the texture that starch confers to meats and dishes accented with it.

The *Analysis of the Han System*[11] said: the state of Qi [in northern Shandong] referred to bran as the matchmaker. The matchmaker should really be the starch.

Choice of Portions

The methods of choosing the right portions of ingredients are as follows: Use pork tenderloin for quick stir-fries, taking the inner muscle of the ham for meatballs, and use pork belly for slow braises. Black carp and grouper are good fish for stir-frying, while grass carp and the common carp are good for making fish floss.[12] Steamed chicken should be made using hens, braised chicken should be made using capons, and chicken broth should be made using mature chickens. For chickens, hens are more tender, while for ducks, drakes are more plump. For water-shield greens (*Brasenia schreberi*, *pocai* 蓴菜 or *chuncai* 純菜) an aquatic plant known for its sticky texture, one uses the tips, while for celery and garlic chives, one uses the lower stems. There are definite reasons for choosing ingredients in these manners, with each ingredient having its own distinctive reasons.

Floss (*song* 鬆) is a dish made of stir-fried, mashed, and dried meat. It has a wooly yet crisp texture. It can be made of fish, pork, chicken, or other meats.

Thresholds

A dish that should be thick and rich should not be so rich that it becomes greasy. A dish that is supposed to be savory and light must not be so light as to taste insipid. When trying to find the thresholds for each criterion, missing by the breadth of a hair can result in the complete failure of a dish. To bring out the essence of a rich dish, one should only clarify the dish to the point of removing just the sediment. If one enjoys a dish simply

---

11 The *Analysis of the Han System* (*Han zhi kao* 漢制考) is a document about political administration during the Han dynasty (206 BCE–220 CE). It is attributed to the Southern Song scholar Wang Yinglin 王應麟 (1223–1296).

12 It is interesting that the fish mentioned here are slightly different from those in the fish floss recipe in the chapter "Water Tribe".

for its rich oiliness, one might as well dine on lard. To bring out the true flavors of a light dish, one should refine the dish only so that distracting flavors are removed. If one demands utterly light flavors, one might as well drink water.

Clarification is a cooking technique that removes all solids and particulates in a liquid. This typically involves the addition of ingredients such as egg white, blood, or pounded meats to a cooking liquid. This is similar to the process used in Western cuisine to make consommé.

Rescuing Dishes

A chef of the utmost caliber can create a dish with every element seasoned and cooked to perfection, never needing to rescue any dish from failure. For the sake of the common chef, however, we shall speak about how to save a failing dish.

When seasoning a dish, one prefers to fail by making it too bland rather than too salty. A bland dish can be rescued by adding more salt, but an overly salty dish cannot be made less salty.[13] When cooking fish, one would rather have it be undercooked than overcooked. An undercooked fish can be further cooked to doneness, while an overcooked fish cannot be reversed and made less cooked. To figure this out, one simply needs to carefully watch one's cooking technique when preparing a dish.

Foundations

Manchu cuisine has more roasted and stewed dishes, Han cuisine tends to have more soup-based dishes. When one is exposed to a culture's foundations and trained in its methods from a young age, one can become extremely adept in the culture's cuisine.

As such, when a Han hires a Manchu or a Manchu hires a Han to prepare the cuisines for which they are most adept, the resulting dishes are a delight to eat, completely devoid of the jarring, confused qualities of poor imitations. Sadly, people today have forgotten the importance of this truth. Rather, they prefer to only

---

13 Actually, this is not completely true. For stews and soups, one could just add more stock and ingredients, though it depends on how over-salted a dish actually is.

ingratiate themselves with the other at the expense of the cuisine. When a Han invites a Manchu to eat Manchu food, or a Manchu invites a Han to eat Han food, what is served is a sad pastiche of the other culture's cuisine, prepared without the fundamental techniques, much like a person trying to paint a tiger but ending up with a mangy dog.[14]

This is the same for scholars taking their examinations; namely, each scholar should make full use of their foundational skills and experiences during the exam, writing in his own words. By consistently following this method, favorable results will come. If a scholar, however, is always trying to imitate the style of every master that he comes upon or the calligraphy of every chief examiner he is trying to please, this person's knowledge will forever be only skin deep, lacking in both depth and substance. Such an individual will never achieve anything in life.

---

14 Most people do this with good intentions, but when Western friends take me to the "*best* Chinese restaurant in town," it most often ends up being a disappointment. I'm absolutely sure I've done likewise for other cuisines.

Food for the Ears and Eyes

One of Yuan Mei's biggest pet peeves was meals for the ears and the eyes, or dishes solely prepared for the purpose of impressing the guests with fancy ingredients and a stunning appearance, but with little flavor. Chinese emperors had a lot of "dishes for the eyes" in their official meals that were designed to show their wealth and power, and to serve as metaphor and invocation for the continued wealth and prosperity of the country. Most of the dishes served during these official meals were never touched or they were given to underlings to show that they were still in the emperor's favor. Many emperors were reported to have eaten rather simple meals in their private quarters, even, shockingly, plain rice congee. Dishes for the ears are also a mainstay of gastronomy, be it in Eastern or Western cuisine. Foie gras is fantastic, but if a restaurant serves it too thin (less than five millimeters thick) just to be able to mention it on a menu, that's an ear meal. White truffle oil (usually containing no truffle shavings whatsoever) in your pasta? Ear meal. "Kobe beef" hamburgers? Yet another ear meal.

Objectionables

Politicians like to boast of the fabulous things they have created. Truth be told, it would be better if they could just resolve preexisting problems. Likewise, if one could eliminate undesirable culinary habits, one would have already made much headway into understanding cuisine. Assembled here is the list of objectionables.

Dousing with Oil

When preparing a dish, a vulgar chef will typically have a simmering pot of rendered lard ready to douse the finished dish before serving, just to impart some richness to it.[1] Even something as light and delicate as bird's nest would not be spared this polluting offense. Then there are those vulgar, ignorant people, with their long, greedy tongues and teeth, who would gladly gulp down these dishes doused with liquid grease. Perhaps they were reincarnated from a bunch of hungry ghosts.[2]

Mixed Pot Cookery

The offensive problem of cooking by mixing everything in a pot has already been addressed previously in the Essential Knowledge section "Transformations."[3]

Meals for the Ears

What are "meals for the ears"? Meals for the ears exist only for bolstering name and reputation. By boasting the names of expensive and coveted ingredients, flaunting one's wealth to esteemed guests, such meals tease one's ears but confer no satisfaction to one's tongue.

Don't they know that the flavors of well-seasoned tofu excel that of bird's nest, and that badly prepared delicacies of the sea cannot match vegetables and bamboo shoots? In the past I have

---

1 It appears that Yuan Mei was not against finishing dishes with a drizzle of oil (for example, when a fish has been steamed to perfection and garnished with shredded green onions, it is quite nice to top it with some sizzling hot sesame oil mixed with cooking oil), but he probably objected to the often-practiced (even today) ladling of a large amount of fat onto a finished dish.

2 See a modern incarnation of these hungry ghosts at your local all-you-can-eat Chinese buffet.

3 When it is done well, combining ingredients in one pot can synthesize new and better flavors. Case in point is the famous Fujian dish "Buddha Jumps over the Wall" (Fo tioa qiang 佛跳牆), in which numerous ingredients such as dried scallops, dry-cured ham, mushrooms, chicken, shark's fin, bamboo shoots, and sea cucumber are steamed together in broth. Through a long cooking process, the discrete flavors of these sometimes unpleasant-smelling ingredients meld together and are transformed and unified into a dish so alluring that it is said that even the followers of Buddha would abandon their temples and their strict vegetarian regime to partake in it.

often referred to chicken, pork, fish, and duck as the "talented nobility" of food ingredients, because they each have their distinguishing flavors, and they hold a dish together by their own merits and ensure its success. Ingredients such as sea cucumber and bird's nest, on the other hand, are more akin to those vulgar and despicable individuals of society who are devoid of spirit and character and mostly reliant on the support and merits of others to succeed.[4]

I once attended a certain prefecture banquet, where we were served bowls as big as tureens, each filled with four taels of bird's nest cooked in plain water.[5] It had not a shred of flavor, yet the guests were clamoring to praise it. To this I joked, "I came here to enjoy bird's nest, not to deal in it wholesale!" Tell me, what exactly is the purpose of serving pricey food at a banquet in such large portions if it tastes terrible? If the sole expressed purpose of this exercise is to flaunt one's wealth and position, one might as well fill the banquet bowls with hundreds of gleaming pearls worth tens of thousands in gold taels. It would be just as inedible and pointless.

Meals for the Eyes

What are "meals for the eyes"? Meals for the eyes exist only to satisfy one's desire to see large quantities and varieties of food. Present-day people are most impressed when the banquet table is overladen with food-filled dishes and bowls of every size, which are undoubtedly great for viewing but not made for tasting.

---

4 By making an analogy between expensive delicacies and despicable characters, and between common ingredients and noble individuals, one cannot help but read this as Yuan Mei's critique of the imperial ruling elite and his support for imperial officials of the scholarly classes—no doubt informed by his own experiences as an official. For him, the elites, while admired and held in high esteem, often claim the effort of others as their own even while they are completely dependent on them for their success and sustenance. This is similar to sea cucumber, bird's nest, and shark's fin. While luxurious and coveted in Chinese cuisine, they require excellent broths made from ham, chicken, and numerous "unsung heroes" to bolster their flavors and make them edible.

5 This must have been an extravagant affair, considering that bird's nest is usually served in small dessert bowls. Even in this day and age, when bird's nest is more accessible and easily (over) harvested, 150 grams of bird's nest per person is still quite a large quantity. In early 2014, 150 grams of medium-quality bird's nest cost around US$225. Top grade is easily double that price.

Chinese emperors had a lot of "dishes for the eyes" in their official meals to show their wealth and power, partly to serve as metaphor and invocation for the continued wealth and prosperity of the country. Most of the dishes served during these official meals were never touched or they were given to underlings to show that they were still in the emperor's favor. Many emperors were reported to have eaten rather simple meals in their private quarters, even, shockingly, plain rice congee.

One must understand that even the best calligraphers will fault if they overextend themselves in writing, and the most renowned poets will invariably compose tired verses when vexed. Note that even through great effort, an excellent chef can produce only four or five good dishes over the course of a day, not to mention the fact that the success of an individual dish is not guaranteed.

Therefore, can we really expect much of the food if a chef had to throw together enough of it to cover a banquet table? Even with numerous helpers in the kitchen, each of the helpers has different skill levels and opinions on how things should be done; as such, the more of them there are, the worse the dishes usually become.

I once attended a banquet hosted by a merchant, where three separate courses were served along with sixteen appetizers. In total, the banquet amounted to almost forty dishes! While the host was immensely satisfied with the pompous banquet, I left it hungry and had to prepare congee at home to quell my hunger. Such banquets, while abundant with food, are both vulgar and unwholesome. The calligrapher Kong Linzhi of the Southern Dynasties period once said, "People of present times enjoy numerous foods, but few of them are for the mouth, and most of them for the eyes." I would only add that if the grand spread of dishes before oneself is rank and unpleasant, no pleasure can be derived on viewing it.

Exaggeration

Each ingredient has its innate characteristics that are best shown off using a specific set of culinary techniques. One must not "force" an ingredient using techniques that exaggerate or overextend these characteristics. Bird's nest is delectable the way it is, so why would one wish to pound and shape it into balls?[6] Sea cucumbers are fine in their original form, so why would one wish to turn them into sauce? One knows that sliced watermelon quickly loses its delicate freshness if left out too long, yet some would go so far as to process it into cakes and pastries. Similarly, cooked apples lose their crispness, yet there are those who would steam and dry them.

Then there are pastries such as wisteria biscuits, described in the almanac *Eight Works on Honoring Life*[7] and magnolia cakes described by Li Liweng, all of them examples of ingredients forcefully bent and twisted out of their normal character. It would be as if one tried to make cups and bowls out of willow twigs—a rather sorry and futile exercise. If sincere people of great virtue can attain sainthood on their own at home, why would they wish to hide this fact?[8]

Delays

To get the most of a dish's flavor, it is best to serve it as soon as it has been removed from the wok and plated. Consuming food that has been sitting around can be likened to wearing an old mildewed robe: even one made of the finest material and finished with the most exquisite details will not make it more enjoyable or smell better.

Some banquet hosts are rather impatient in nature, insisting that all dishes must be brought to the table at the same time. To

---

6 For some truly ridiculous bird's nest dishes, watch the original Japanese *Iron Chef* 料理の鉄人 episode "Swallow's Nest Battle" (season 3, episode 29, originally aired 21 July 1995), where Chen Kenichi goes against Li Jinlun.

7 *Eight Works on Honoring Life* (*Zunsheng Bajian* 遵生八箋), written during the Ming dynasty by Gao Lian, is an eight-volume (nineteen-scroll) almanac on lifestyle and well-being that covers a wide range of subjects, from classic Chinese arts, to medicinal concoctions and curatives, to travelling and living. Interestingly, the recipe for *wisteria* biscuits mentioned here is actually not in this work, which means that Yuan Mei made an error either in the name of the literary source or the recipe itself.

8 In Chinese folktales, in order to attain sainthood, a person had to climb to the peak of a mystical mountain and become the apprentice of a saint with a long white beard, being tested in trials and undergoing years of physical and psychological struggle. Becoming a saint in the comfort of one's home was infinitely tamer and less extraordinary. What Yuan Mei is trying to indicate here is that one should not be ashamed of cooking an ingredient in the canonical way just because the technique is simple or common.

The famous Aijia or Ai pear 哀家梨 has been lauded in literature since the Han dynasty (206 BCE–220 CE) for its large size and remarkably crisp yet tender texture. This contrasts with the more common Asian pear, the Ya pear, which, although crunchy, tends to be much tougher and thus is sometimes steamed before eating. The Chinese idiom "steaming Ai pears for eating" (*aili zhengshi* 哀梨蒸食) is used to describe foolish people who have no idea of the quality of a thing and thus proceed to ruin it. It is similar to the Western idiom "casting pearls before swine."

make this happen, the kitchen staff would prepare all of the banquet's dishes beforehand, keep them warm in a steamer, and await the signal from the host to bring them all to the table. Can these dishes be expected to have any flavor left after such a long delay?

It should be noted that a good chef toils to perfect the details in every bowl and dish of food produced, but when the food gets to the people who eat, it is violently swallowed without tasting, regardless of its state. This is as wasteful as if one received some delectably crisp Aijia pears and insisted that they be steamed for eating.

While traveling in Guangdong Province, I had Magistrate Yang Lanpo's incredibly good rice-eel soup. When I inquired on the secret to making a dish so perfect, I was told, "The eel was killed and cooked to your order and served the moment it is done without delay. That is all." This principle should be applied to all aspects of food preparation and serving.

Waste

Tyrannical individuals are not empathetic to people's labors, just as wasteful individuals care little about the value of things. From head to tail, all parts of a chicken, fish, goose, or duck are delicious in their own way. As such, there is no need to carve out the best part of something only to relegate the rest as waste. One often sees soft-shell turtle prepared by portioning off the "skirt"[9] while the rest of the turtle with its fragrant meat is discarded. It is also

---

9 The "shell" of a soft-shell turtle is actually covered in skin and is hard only in the center. The edges of this dome are a fatty and fleshy "skirt" that many consider the choice portion of a soft-shell turtle.

not uncommon to see the belly of a shad sliced off and reserved for steaming without considering that the best flavor comes from its dorsal parts.[10] By far the most common example of pointless waste can be found in some chefs' preparations of salted eggs. The yolk of a salted egg is unarguably its best part, with its white ranking a distant second. But discard the whites and serve only the yolk, and the eating experience would not feel half as enjoyable.[11]

This is not to say that I champion the commoner's ideas of conserving every part of an ingredient. Quite the opposite; if "wasting" part of an ingredient can greatly enhance the resulting dish, then all the better.[12] But if one purposefully discards the portions of an ingredient to the detriment of a dish, then what is the point indeed?

As for the practice of roasting the feet of live geese or cutting out the liver of a live chicken for the sake of gastronomy, such are foods that a gentleman should never partake. Why? Taking the life of a creature for food can be justified, but doing so in a way that it begs for death is unjustifiable.[13]

Indulging in Drink

Only one who is alert can tell the difference between right and wrong. Likewise, only one who is mindful can discern the differences between good and bad flavors. The famous chef Yi Yin observed, "The profound nuances of flavor cannot be rightly expressed in words." If a drunkard cannot even speak, how can

---

10 Reeves shad is chock-full of spiny bones.

11 Although the layer of toppings on the pizza is the most flavorful, eating it on its own would be far less enjoyable.

12 Almost all parts of animals can be eaten, or used for preparation, save the gall bladders, gills, horns, hooves, and teeth. Meat aside, the bones make great stock, tendons are delectable when stewed, and cartilage makes interesting cold dishes with enjoyable textures.

13 While this is not the first recorded instance of Chinese animal welfare activism, one could say that Yuan Mei was an animal rights advocate, not to mention a decent person. Judging by the rhetorical question he asks ("Why?"), it appears that such dishes were not uncommon at the lavish feasts attended by those who would consider themselves "gentlemen." This sadistic habit likely stemmed from a perversion of the idea of avoiding delays. After all, what can be fresher and more nutritious than meat cut from an animal while it is still alive? Sadly, such inhumane practices can still be found in East Asia, for example in "live sashimi."

there be any hope that he can express, much less discern, the flavors of anything?

Every so often, I see people playing drinking games during banquets, their minds clouded and absent from having had too much alcohol. In such inebriated states, those great dishes they are eating might as well be sawdust. The heads of those preoccupied with drinking are somewhere else entirely, with their faculties for judging food swept out the door. If one really must indulge in drink, first have a proper meal where the dishes can be tasted, then only afterward bring out the alcohol. In this way, you get the best of both worlds.

Chafing Dishes

In Yuan Mei's time, chafing dishes were heated vessels to keep food warm, but the Chinese name, *huoguo* 火鍋 (lit., fire pot) is used today to describe a hot pot, a large pot with hot soup or stock where ingredients are briefly boiled in directly at the table by the diners themselves. Yuan Mei did not oppose to preparing food in a hot pot, although in a later chapter he does mention it tends to lack flavor.

Chafing dishes are often used when hosting banquets in winter, which is a rather irritating practice considering how noisy they are. This is not to overlook the more serious problem of their use, ignoring the fact that cooking a dish with optimal flavor requires the precise control of heat and the duration of its application.[14]

Recently people have started using alcohol-based chafing dishes instead of charcoal, believing them to be an improvement. This is not the case. Regardless of the type, the use of chafing dishes will lead to overcooked food that has changed its flavor for the worse. Some people may contest, "But what if the food gets cold?"

I would say to them, "If that boiled thing just scooped out of the pot does not whet the guests' appetite, then let them eat it cold so they know how bad it really tastes."

14 See also the section devoted to the topic of heat control (*huo hou* 火候) in the "Essential Knowledge" chapter.

Imposition

A banquet host extends his courtesy and generosity toward his guests by providing them with good food. But once the food is laid out on the table, the guests should be allowed to choose whatever food they fancy, regardless of whether it is refined, oily, cut in chunks, or chopped into bits. A person of reason attends to the preferences of his guests; therefore, why would he wish to impose his own?

It is all too common to see annoying hosts endlessly piling food up on their guests' dishes and bowls until they overflow.[15] It is not as if these guests are missing their hands or eyes, nor are they young children or new brides graciously holding back out of modesty, so why would hosts emulate something done by crass old dames from the countryside? In doing so, they play a poor host by deliberately ignoring the wishes of their guests! Recently, I have seen even more despicable manners, where a host would go so far as violating his guests' person by insistently shoving chopsticks full of food into their mouths!

In Chang'an there was a man who loved entertaining guests but tended to serve rather mediocre food at his banquets. During an occasion, one of his guests asked, "Are we good friends?" to which the man replied, "Of course!" The guest then dropped to his knees begging, "If we are indeed good friends, then I have a request to make and will not stand until you agree to it." Astonished the man asked, "What is it?" to which the guest replied, "When you host banquets in the future, I beg you to not invite me." There were roars of laughter all around, as they all sat down.

Rendering Fat

Although ingredients such as fish, pork, chicken, and duck can be rather fatty in nature, it is nevertheless imperative that most of their fat be retained within the meat itself and not be allowed to

---

15 Many of us who were immersed in traditional Chinese culture in our formative years are too often guilty of this behavior.

render out into the cooking stock to prevent its flavor from being diluted. If this fat becomes rendered, what flavor the meat could have had will be leached into the stock.[16]

There are three bad culinary techniques that result in fat being rendered from meat: First, the cooking heat was too high, and extra water had to be added to restore the amount of cooking liquid in the food. Second, the cooking flames were stopped, only to be resumed later after a long pause. And finally, an impatient chef who continually checks the doneness of food as it is cooking results in the lid being opened numerous times throughout the process, which inevitably leads to the rendering of fat from the meat.

Clichés

Although commonly (mis-)translated as "snack," small delicacies (*xiaochi* 小吃) in Chinese cuisine are more like small, quick-to-eat dishes than a snack in the modern Western sense. A hot dog or poutine would be more akin to a *xiaochi* in Chinese cuisine than a bag of potato chips.

Tang poetry is deemed to be the pinnacle of classical poetry, yet the poetic form is seldom referred to or quoted by famous poets.[17] Why? Because of its widespread and popular use, the material has become hopelessly cliché.[18] If this can be true with poetry, so, too, can it be true for gastronomy.

In today's imperial court cuisine, one too often hears of ostentatious references to "sixteen dishes, eight vessels, and four side dishes," the "Manchu-Han banquet," the "eight small delicacies," or the "ten great dishes." These hackneyed categories stem from the vulgar habits of bad chefs. Displays this trite are useful only for welcoming new relations through the gates or when a superior comes to

---

16 The intramuscular fat in meat makes it tasty and juicy. This is the reason that Kobe beef or highly marbled meats should be served rare or very lightly cooked.

17 The poetic "five syllables, eight rhyme poetry," form refers to a regulated verse consisting of eight lines with five syllables per line, originating in China during the Tang dynasty (618–907 CE) and popular throughout East Asia. It is also known as the Imperial Examination poetic form (*shi tie shi* 試帖詩) because of its use in the Chinese imperial examinations over several dynastic periods.

18 This is like Beethoven's piano piece "Für Elise", which has been played so often as background in elevators and children's recitals worldwide that it has lost nearly all impact.

visit. They serve as perfunctory acts of duty: mere decorations to be set next to tables and chairs draped in embroideries, fine ornamental screens, and embellished incense platforms.[19] Of course, all this is to be accompanied by one's endless bowing as required by custom.

If one is having a celebratory banquet at one's abode, where the grand meal will be interwoven with prose, poetry, and fine *jiu*, how could one feel comfortable hosting it in manners as trite as those mentioned above? When feasting with close friends and kin, the foods need to be assembled together in a joyous disarray of dishes and bowls such that an intimate air of refinement is brought to the meal.

Birthday and wedding banquets in my family tend to become rather large affairs that gather enough guests to easily fill five or six tables. On these occasions, outside chefs need to be hired, which inevitably leads to the food becoming the aforementioned sad and ostentatious displays. If the hired chefs, however, are in fact skilled and experienced, capable of preparing the dishes to my specifications, then the resulting food is quite something else altogether.[20]

Muddiness

Just because a dish is muddy and turbid doesn't mean that its texture will be thick and unctuous. Soups that resemble silted water from an agitated barrel or broths the color of gray liquids from a dyeing vat—neither of them have appearances and flavors that anyone could enjoy.

The way to rescue turbid and muddy dishes is as follows: rinse all the solid ingredients well, prudently adjust the amount of seasonings, add the right quantities of water, cook at the right heat, and correct the salty and sourness of the food. Importantly, the resulting dish should not coat the mouth of the diner with an unpleasant film.

---

19 In modern Chinese society, these things are brought out during days of worship, like the Taiwanese *da bai bai* 大拜拜 day when ancestors and deities are venerated.

20 It almost seems that in this paragraph, Yuan Mei excuses himself from any clichéd banquets he may have hosted. The last sentence is a boast of his own gastronomic, if not culinary, prowess.

The Liang dynasty poet Yu Xin stated in his poetry, "Those who tremble lack inner strength. Those with confused characters have vulgar hearts,"[21] which perfectly describes the character of such muddied dishes.

Sloppiness

Sloppiness should not be tolerated for any task, including matters of gastronomy. Chefs are uncultured people of lowly upbringing; thus, if one does not properly reward or punish them, they will begin taking shortcuts and become negligent of their culinary duties. Should you willingly ingest the barely cooked vegetables you were served today, you can be sure they will be served raw to you tomorrow. If you hold your tongue when you are served ruined food, then the dishes served next time will be thrown together even more haphazardly.

Furthermore, one should not just reward and punish a chef without context. Dishes that were well executed should be identified and praised. Conversely, dishes that were done poorly should be investigated and interrogated upon. The standards of flavors in a dish must be stringently upheld, and deviations must not be allowed. Likewise, the length and intensity of the heat used in preparing a dish must never be left to the whims of the chef but must be explicitly prescribed. Chefs who take shortcuts and diners who do not care: such are the factors that are detrimental to food and cuisine.

Interrogation, introspection, and understanding: these are the principles of building knowledge. Providing timely advice to students and lessons that are sufficiently challenging: such are the principles of being a teacher. Should this not also be true for cuisine?[22]

---

21 This is a line from the poem "In Imitation of 'Singing My Cares'" (Ni yong huai 擬詠懷), in which Yu Xin laments having been sent to the northern capital of Chang'an:

Flavorless, flavorless, lacking true qi

Muddled, muddled, having vulgar hearts

It is used here to indicate that a dish must not be turbid in order to have impact and character in both appearance and flavor.

22 This section is modeled after the traditional scholarly discourse on rewards and punishments as tools to shape behavior.

Ocean and River Delicacies:
From Bird's Nest to Imitation Crab

Starting off with bird's nest and shark's fin, and covering more delicacies from the rivers and seas, these chapters can be seen as Yuan Mei's effort to show the best of what Chinese gastronomy has to offer. These ingredients were considered exotic, exclusive, and expensive, which made them prized for important meals. The preparation of the ingredients is a good introduction to the effort, refinement, and skills required of a high caliber Chinese chef.

The Chinese terms *haixian* 海鲜 and *jiangxian* 江鲜 mean savory items from the sea/river. A common translation is "seafood" or "freshwater fish," but doing this would exclude the air of luxury and exoticism of the ingredients introduced in this chapter: bird's nest, sea cucumbers, shark's fin, and abalone. Instead, "ocean and river delicacies" is far more accurate, especially since later chapters include recipes with more common seafood and shellfish, while these chapters do cover the more rare ingredients.

As Yuan Mei notes, the ancient Chinese rulers who held power were overwhelmingly inland people; thus the lack of emphasis on food from the ocean in older sources is not surprising. This focus extended well into the later dynasties, and the rarity of seafood in the diets of most Chinese people added to this sense of luxury and exclusivity. This is also evident from the Chinese phrase for general culinary delicacies: treasures from the mountains, flavors of the oceans (*shanzhen haiwei* 山珍海味). Simply mentioning these treasures from the sea is sufficient to invoke the exotic.

OCEAN DELICACIES

The eight delicacies referred to by the ancients made no mention of seafood. These days, however, one cannot avoid following the will of the masses. Assembled here are the recipes with ocean delicacies.

Bird's Nest

Bird's nests are constructed by the swift species *Aerodramus maximus* and *Aerodramus fuciphagus* as they progressively layer their saliva into a crescent half-bowl form. The nests have been harvested sustainably for much of history, however a combination of economic and environmental factors have resulted in steadily decreasing populations of these swift species. Bird's nests in raw form are firm but friable and although they consist mainly of the dried saliva protein, they still contain feathers and specks of dust that require thorough cleaning prior to preparation. The methods described by Yuan Mei are still the most common and favored for preparation of bird's nest.

Bird's nest is an expensive ingredient, but it should not be used in small amounts. If one wishes to serve bird's nest, each bowl must contain at least two *liang* of the ingredient, prepared by first soaking it in boiled rainwater, with any dark strands or debris removed using a needle. It must then be boiled in a soup made of the broths of tender chickens, good ham, and young mushrooms until the bird's nest takes on the tone and translucency of jade. Note that bird's nest is extremely delicate in flavor and must not be prepared with anything greasy. Its soft and elegant texture also necessitates that it is never combined with foods that are firm or aggressive in taste.

People today like to serve bird's nest with shredded pork and chicken. In doing this, they taste only shredded chicken and pork, not bird's nest.

In a futile effort to feign wealth, some hosts would scatter three *qian* of raw bird's nest as a thin facade on top of a bowl of soup. One could have picked them out like wisps of gray hair.[1] These shreds of bird's

A *qian* 錢 is a traditional measurement. One *qian* equals about 3.7 grams.

---

1 The phrase "wisps of gray hair" may have come from a similar expression that originated from the poem "My Worries Are as Numerous as My Grey Hairs" by the Tang dynasty poet Gu Kuang 顧 況 in his compendium *Guishan Zuo* 歸山作. The full poem goes:

My worries are as numerous as my grey hairs
My past life vast as the grey distant mountains.
In the empty woods the falling snow keeps me company.
On the old deserted road I make my journey home.

nest immediately disappear when a guest stirs their bowl, revealing it full of only coarse ingredients. Like the ruse of a beggar child pretending to be rich, this only reveals how poor they actually are.

If, for whatever reason, one must add anything else to the bird's nest soup, use shredded mushrooms,[2] shredded bamboo shoot tips, fish maw, or slices of pheasant breast. During my visit to Yangming Prefecture, Guangdong [Province], I had an incredibly good winter melon and bird's nest. It was richly flavored with only chicken and mushroom extracts, the soft textures and delicate flavors of the two main ingredients matching each other superbly.

Bird's nest should have the tone and translucency of jade, and it should never be opaque white. Those who make bird's nest into balls and pound it into powder are doing nothing but concocting strained interpretations of the ingredient.[3]

Three Ways of Preparing Sea Cucumbers

As an ingredient, sea cucumbers have little to no taste, are full of sand, and are remarkably fishy in smell.[4] For these reasons, they are also the most difficult ingredient to prepare well.

Because it is by nature thick and heavy in texture and flavor, sea cucumber should never be cooked in mild and delicate soups. For small spiked sea cucumbers, one must first soak them in water

Sea cucumbers (*Holothuria*), known in Chinese as "ginseng of the ocean" are almost never sold fresh. When dried, they are hard as a rock and should be a bit heavy for their size. After being scrubbed, boiled, and stewed until tender and infused with a rich broth, they are delectable savory, with a unique, springy texture.

Perhaps in writing this, Yuan Mei is trying to convey the feelings of loneliness and dejection he felt wanting to eat a bowl of bird's nest soup but finding only a soup sprinkled with wisps of it.

2 Here, Yuan Mei does not mean shiitake, since their dark skin would clash with the bird's nest. Rather, he likely means the common button mushroom (*Agaricus bisporus*) or the white mushroom (e.g., *Coprinus comatus* [shaggy mane, also known as chicken drumstick mushroom]), which are both mentioned in other parts of the text.

3 In other words, don't overstretch the "capabilities" of your ingredients.

4 With a description like this, one likely wonders why anyone would bother to cook, much less eat, sea cucumber. While some may eat it for purported male enhancement effects or its high collagen content, connoisseurs will pay top dollar to experience the pleasure that only sea cucumbers can provide.

to remove all the mud and sand embedded within them.[5] The sea cucumbers must then be boiled three times in meat broth, then afterward simmered in chicken and pork extracts with soy sauce until soft. One should use shiitake or wood ear mushrooms as supporting ingredients to sea cucumber since their colors match well. If one is entertaining guests the next day, preparations for the sea cucumbers must be started immediately since they need to be simmered for an entire day in order to be soft enough to eat.

During the summer, Observer Qian's household serves an exceptionally good salad of shredded sea cucumber tossed with dressing made with ground mustard and chicken extract, and a soup of finely diced sea cucumber with diced bamboo shoots and diced shiitake mushrooms in chicken broth. In the household of Assistant Minister Jiang, they serve a very good dish made with simmered tofu sheets, chicken thighs, and mushrooms with sea cucumbers.

Two Ways of Preparing Shark's Fin

Shark's fin does not soften easily and needs to be boiled for about two days before it is supple enough to eat. There are two ways of preparing shark's fin: The first involves simmering it with good ham, good chicken broth, fresh bamboo shoots, and a few grams of rock sugar. The second way uses only chicken broth and

Shark's fin is the cartilaginous part of the fin and is usually sold dried and skinned. When properly prepared, shark's fin is smooth and supple, with a tender snap when one bites into it. In Traditional Chinese Medicine, it is seen as a strengthening food, due in part to its high protein and mineral content. For festive occasions, shark's fin is therefore served both for good health and for culinary delight. Today, this custom should be discouraged, since rising demand is driving unsustainable fishing practices, threatening the survival of many shark's species.

---

5 The Japanese sea cucumbers (*Apostichopus japonicas*) mentioned here are small, spiky, and popular for individual servings due to their size. But for many gourmets, *Holothuria fuscogilva*, commonly known as the white teatfish, is more alluring for the thickness of its gelatinous flesh. Thickness is a desirable quality that extends to many other ingredients, including squid, cuttlefish, and wood-ear mushrooms.

finely shredded radish and pulls the shark's fin apart into shreds. When cooked, both radish and shark's fin meld together in the bowl such that a diner cannot tell one apart from the other. The recipe using the ham has less liquid, while the one using radish has more.

A well-prepared shark's fin must be harmoniously balanced in it smoothness and suppleness. If one serves sea cucumber that flicks one's nose and shark's fin that bounces off the plate, it would be told as a joke among one's guests. When Daoist Wu serves shark's fin at home, his chefs do not use the bottom scale-containing portions and prefer to use only the upper half of the fin's roots, a rather unique method of preparation.[6] The shredded radish must be immersed and soaked in water three times in order to remove its odor. I have also tasted the shark's fin and vegetables stir-fry at the home of Guo Gengli, which was superb! It is too bad they did not pass on the technique for preparing this dish.[7]

Abalone

Abalone is best when thinly sliced and stir-fried. The household of Yang Zhongcheng serves a dish called "abalone tofu," where abalone is shaved tinly and simmered in a soup of chicken broth, tofu, and seasoned with aged lees sauce. Prefect Zhuang serves a very unique dish consisting of large chunks of abalone braised with duck. Abalone, however, is quite firm and tough and must be braised for three days before it is tender enough to eat.[8]

> Lees sauce or wine lees sauce (*zaoyou* 糟油) is made by ageing a mixture of wine lees, Shaoxing *jiu*, sugar, salt, and osmanthus flowers.

---

6 This sentence is slightly puzzling since sharks technically don't have scales. Yuan Mei likely meant the scale-like skin denticles on the shark's fin.

7 This last phrase could also be translated as "decided not to share"; that is, shared it with Yuan Mei when he asked the Guo household.

8 The abalone referred to in this section is likely the dried form, as that is much tougher after rehydration and takes a bit of cooking to soften. Fresh abalone can be grilled or steamed and eaten straight out of the shell, and while it is chewy, it is not tough.

Mussels

Mussels come in dried or fresh form, but since Yuan Mei lived inland, the mussels he used were most likely dried.

Braising pork with mussels in broth produces a dish that is incredibly savory. Remove the innards of the mussel and one can make a good stir-fry flavored with *jiu* using the reserved flesh.

Whitebait

Whitebait are small dried fish from Ningbo in Zhejiang Province. Their flavor is similar to that of dried shrimp and is very good in steamed egg.[9] They make excellent side dishes.

Cuttlefish Roe

Cuttlefish roe is very savory and delicious but also difficult to prepare. One needs to thoroughly boil it using river water to remove any sand and rid it of its stench. After that, it must be simmered with chicken broth and mushrooms until tender. Marshall Gong Yun-ruo's household prepares this dish most skillfully.

This roe is most likely mullet roe, also known by its Japanese name *karasumi*. It is the nidamental gland (the egg and egg-cac producing organ) of the cuttlefish.

Scallops

Scallops come from Ningbo and should be prepared in the same manner as cockles (ridge-shelled family *Arcidae*) and razor clams (elongated rectangular shells of the *Ensis* or *Solen* genus).[10] The most delicious and crisp portion of the scallop is the central

---

9 This works best with small shrimp, only two to three millimeters wide. The larger kind (wider than four millimeters) are better stir-fried and used as a side dish or a snack with some drinks.

10 Well-made dried scallops are much richer in taste than the fresh item. The cockles here is most likely *Tegillarca granosa*, known in Chinese as the "silver cockle" (*yinhan* 銀蚶) due to its bright white shell. The of cockles indicated here is most likely *Solen strictus*, which has been farmed extensively in the mud flats of coastal areas of China.

"pillar." Thus when shucking scallop, one will be throwing away most of it and keeping only this small portion.

Oysters

Oysters grow with their shells stuck fast to rocks, making them particularly difficult to dislodge. After being shucked, they can be cooked as a thick soup in the same manner as cockles and clams. Known also as "ghost eyes,"[11] oysters can only be found in the two prefectures of Yueqing and Fenghua and nowhere else.[12]

> This kind of thick soup or stew (*geng* 羹) is made by adding potato, corn, or arrowroot starch to a clear broth, giving it a silky texture.

---

11 The reason for this strange name could be because boiled oysters plump into an eyeball shape and appear somewhat ghostlike.

12 Oysters are available in both fresh and dried form. The former is common around coastal regions, while the latter is available in most parts of China and in Chinese dried-food stores (*haiwei ganhuo* 海味乾貨) around the world. It is not known why Yuan Mei states that oysters can only be found in these two prefectures. Perhaps Yueqing and Fenghua were the only places in the Qing dynasty that cultivated oysters. It may very well have been that Yuan Mei did not know that oysters grow and can be grown wherever there are clean coastal waters.

RIVER DELICACIES

The ancient scholar Guo Pu's work *Endowments of the River* provides an exhaustive list of fish species. Here, however, I will only mention the more common ones. Assembled here is a list of recipes with river delicacies.

Two Ways of Preparing Grenadier Anchovy[1]

Grenadier anchovy is best when cooked in the manner of shad: seasoned with sweet *jiu* lees and light soy sauce, then placed on a plate and steamed. One does not need to add water in preparing the dish. If one dislikes having to deal with fish bones, use a sharp knife to fillet the fish, then pull out the bones with tweezers. Simmer these fillets in a broth of ham, chicken, and bamboo shoots, and one gets an incredibly delicious soup.

People in Nanjing do not wish to deal with fish bones, so instead they fry the anchovies in oil until they are dried and shriveled and then pan-fry them more afterward.[2] There is an adage that goes "Straighten a humpbacked person's back and you'll surely kill him," which suitably describes this technique.

Madam Tai from the city of Wuhu has another way of preparing this fish. A sharp knife is used to obliquely slice down the back of each grenadier anchovy to sever the bones. They are then pan-fried until golden brown and seasoned with the proper condiments when done. One would be hard-pressed to feel any bones when eating anchovies prepared so.

Reeves shad's life cycle is similar to that of salmon in that the fish grows to adulthood in the sea but spawns in freshwater, justifying its inclusion in this "River Delicacies" section.

Shad

Shad can be steamed with sweet honey *jiu*, but is even better when prepared in the same manner as grenadier anchovy.

---

1 The Chinese name *daoyu* 刀魚 (knife fish) is used to refer to at least half a dozen types of fish. Many of them do not fit the bill, not only because they are saltwater fish but also because they have bones that are far too thick and coarse to be "tamed" using the methods described here. As such, we have to assume that the fish described here is actually the *Coilia* genus of anchovies that swim in the Yangtze River: either *Coilia ectenes*, also known as the Japanese grenadier anchovy; *Coilia macrognathos*, the Osbeck's grenadier anchovy (also known as the Yangtze *dao* fish 长江刀鱼); or *Coilia mystus*. All three anchovies are also known as Phoenix-tail fish (*fengweiyu* 鳳尾魚).

2 In this section, we have "two ways" for preparing grenadier anchovies and not three, because the frying method is mentioned only to make fun of people from Nanjing. Although mocked by Yuan Mei here, this preparation is actually quite similar to that of a dish known as *congshao jiyu* 蔥燒鯽魚 (scallion-braised crucian carp), for which the fish is soaked in vinegar, deep-fried, and then stewed in a vinegar sauce. The result is a whole fish that can be eaten with the head, bones, and flesh all crumbling and melting in one's mouth.

This fish is also very good pan-fried with oil and finished with light soy sauce and wine lees. Shad, however, must not be cut into small chunks and cooked in chicken broth. In addition, do not reserve only the belly of the shad and throw away its back; in doing so, one would lose the true flavors of this fish.

Sturgeon[3]

Master Yin Wenduan boasts that he knew best how to prepare sturgeon; truth is, his method produces an over-stewed fish with a thick and muddy flavor.

I had very good stir-fried sturgeon slices at Tang [Jinghan]'s household in Suzhou. Its preparation was as follows: slice the sturgeon's meat, and fry it in oil with *jiu* and autumn sauce for thirty *gun* [ninety

Gun 滾 literally means "to roll" or "to boil." But it is also used as a time measurement, and based on the recipes, roughly equivalent to three seconds.

seconds], then add water and let it return to a boil. When done, plate the sturgeon slices and garnish heavily with soy-pickled cucumber, soy-pickled ginger, and finely chopped green onions.

The actual size of a cup is hard to determine, but based on the volume of standard wine cups and the use of it in the recipes, it could have been somewhere around one hundred milliliter.

Another method of preparation is to parboil the fish in water for ten moments, remove the large bones, and cut the meat into small cubes.[4] Reserve the cartilage and cut it into small cubes.[5] Add the cubed cartilage to chicken broth, then braise them while skimming the broth of any scum that forms. When the cartilage is 80 percent done, add *jiu*, autumn sauce, and the cubed meat, and keep braising

---

3 The Chinese sturgeon (*Acipenser sinensis*) is endangered due to overharvesting, habitat loss, and pollution in the Yangtze River. They are now raised commercially, not for ecological purposes, but rather for the roe, which is processed and exported to Europe and North America as high-grade caviar, often resold under Russian or French labels to obscure its origins.

4 It is unusual to see a fish being parboiled, since the method is usually reserved for heavier meats such as beef or pork. This may indicate that the texture and taste of sturgeon meat is actually more "meat-like" than most fish.

5 This fish is eaten as much for the cartilage as for the meat, much like shark.

until the meat is 20 percent soft. Finish the dish with a generous cup of ginger juice and garnish with green onions, Sichuan pepper, and garlic chives.

Yellow Croaker[6]

Douchi 豆豉 is one of the oldest processed soybean products. It is made of fermented and dried soybeans, and often used to season dishes.

Cut the yellow croaker into small chunks. Marinate with soy sauce and *jiu* for a day and allow to drip dry. Fry the pieces until the sides are golden brown, then add a small cup of Jinhua *douchi* (fermented black soybeans), a bowl of sweet *jiu*, and a small cup of autumn sauce, and boil together. When the sauce is reduced, add sugar, and soy-pickled cucumber and ginger before plating. The flavors of this dish are deep, rich, and delicious.

Another method of preparing yellow croaker is to first pull the meat off the fish, and then combine it with chicken broth to make a thick soup. Lightly season it with sweet soy sauce and thicken with starch before serving this delicious soup. Note that yellow croaker is a heavy-textured and densely flavored fish and should not be cooked using methods reserved for light or delicate ingredients.

---

6 The challenge in determining the English or scientific name for *huangyu* 黃魚 (lit. yellow fish) comes down to the fact that while there are many references to "yellow" fish in Chinese, there are no freshwater river fish known by this name. Many clues point to the saltwater yellow croaker (*Larimichthys crocea*) since it congregates in the brackish waters of the Yangzte delta and estuary in certain seasons. It is also fished year-round and shipped up the river to be sold in both fresh and dried form. Also, the first recipe is remarkably similar to red-cooked yellow croaker (*hongshao huangyu* 紅燒黃魚) and its variant red-cooked yellow croaker with fermented soybeans (*douchi hongshao huangyu* 豆豉紅燒黃花魚). The second recipe basically describes *yellow croaker soup* (*huangyu geng* 黃魚羹). Both recipes are well-loved preparations for the fish even today. The definitive answer comes from a line in the *Suixiju Gastronomic Manual* 隨息居飲食譜 by a close contemporary of Yuan Mei, the Qing dynasty doctor Wang Shixiong 王士雄. In this document, he explicitly states, "Shishou [stone head] fish is known as *huang* fish, and also as *jiang* fish". This effectively links the *Sciaenidae* or croaker fish family (*shitouyu ke* 石首魚科) with the term *huangyu* 黃魚, making *huangyu* a species of croaker and most likely the yellow croaker. But even more interesting is the fact that the *huangyu* is also known colloquially as *jiangyu* 江魚 or "[Yangtze] river fish," which may explain why Yuan Mei placed it in this chapter of river delicacies despite the fact that it is not a freshwater river fish. All of this indicates that the *huangyu* referred to by Yuan Mei is undoubtedly *Larimichthys crocea*, more commonly known as the yellow croaker.

Snakehead Fish[7]

Snakeheads are the most tender fish of all. To prepare, skin the fish and clean out its inedible innards.[8] Separate the fish's liver from the flesh and braise both in chicken broth with three parts *jiu*, two parts water, and one part autumn sauce. Prior to plating, add one large bowl of ginger juice and many stalks of green onion to reduce its fishiness.

Imitation Crab

Boil two yellow croakers and remove their bones. Add four salted raw eggs to the fish. Break the eggs up without mixing them into the fish, and fry everything quickly with oil. Add chicken broth to the mixture, let boil, and then stir in the salted egg until the mixture is even. Finish the dish with shiitake, green onions, ginger juice, and *jiu*. Serve with liberal amounts of vinegar.[9]

---

7 Although the name *banyu* 班魚 (spotted fish) is used for fish in the grouper family, it is also relatively common to use it to refer to the freshwater snakehead fish (*Channa argus, Channa maculata,* or *Channa asiatica* |山斑鱼|). These freshwater fish, native or naturalized to the Yangtze River, are very tender and are braised to make medicinal soups, similar to the above recipe. Judging from the facts that the recipe here is atypical for grouper, the meat of the grouper is firm rather than tender, and groupers are *not* freshwater fish, it seems unlikely that Yuan Mei's *banyu* 班魚 is a spotted fish of the genus *Epinephelus*; rather, it is one of the snake-patterned fish from the *Channa* genus. Added to this, Yuan Mei later refers to grouper as *jiyu* 季魚, discounting the possibility that this is also grouper.

8 Fish intestines (*yuchang* 魚腸) are actually eaten in many Chinese cuisines, including the famous dish "steam-roasted fish intestines" (*zheng ju yuchang* 蒸焗魚腸), which involves scraping and rinsing the fish intestines clean, adding the liver, mixing with eggs and ingredients that suppress the fishiness, and steaming everything.

9 Crabs are elegant in texture and delectable in taste. Although big meaty crabs are popular throughout the world, in China it is the Chinese mitten crab (*da zhaxie* 大閘蟹, *Eriocheir sinensis*) that reigns supreme. Not only is the meat of the Chinese mitten crab sweet and delicate, but when in season, its carapace is filled with copious amounts of creamy golden-orange roe (*xiegao* 蟹糕 and *xiehuang* 蟹黄). Demand for these crabs is high, and the price can be rather steep. This crab substitute imitates the appearance (the gooey yellow and white of the salted egg), textures (flakiness of the fish), and to a lesser extent the flavors (slight fishiness of salted egg) of a shelled and stir-fried Chinese mitten crab. Not mixing the salted eggs in with the fish at this stage gives this dish the uneven white-and-yellow appearance of stir-fried Chinese mitten crab. Some people eat crab with vinegar to cut or complement the crab's fishiness, as well as the belief in Traditional Chinese Medicine that it deflects the "coldness" of crab. In this case, vinegar is required to hide the fact that this "crab" lacks the requisite fishiness.

The Five Tribes

The theory of the Five Elements (wood, fire, earth, metal, water), the Five Phases, and the Five Flavors are guiding principles in traditional Chinese culture, philosophy, and cuisines. The next five chapters can be seen together as representing this idea as well. Each chapter highlights a basic ingredient, from the most respected meat (pork, poetically called "sacrificial animals" by Yuan Mei) to the much less popular beef and mutton dishes, which was primarily associated with Chinese minorities of Central Asian and Mongolian ethnic backgrounds. In the Winged Tribe section, chicken is the primary bird, but it also includes other fowl like pheasants, duck, and geese.

Yuan Mei made a distinction between scaled (fish) and scaleless aquatic creatures, the latter including several dishes using turtle, an ingredient that is to this day an important element of Chinese Traditional Medicine. In the Chinese tradition, nutrition is an integral part of health and well-being, and gastronomy often had close ties to medicinal practices. Again, the five phases and flavors also play an important part in this "traditional" thinking about food that is pervasive and actively used even today.

Finally, Yuan Mei covers a range of vegetable dishes. But don't be fooled: Although the main ingredients are vegetables, beans, or tofu, the dishes are far from vegetarian. They are often paired with meat, flavored with shrimp, or boiled in chicken or beef stock. Some Buddhist traditions prohibited the eating of animals and strong-smelling (and -tasting) vegetables like onions and garlic, a category that is known in Chinese as *su*. On the opposite side are *hun* dishes and ingredients, which can contain meat and other animal products. Still, vegetarianism as we know it today—for ethical, moral, or environmental reasons—wasn't common. That said, for most of Chinese history, meat was expensive and a luxury item reserved for the richer households. Therefore, simple vegetable dishes with small amounts of meat were very common, and Yuan Mei was often impressed by the simplicity (and, in his eyes, the superiority) of these meals.

A Note on Pork

The Chinese name for this chapter, *tesheng* 特牲, means "special sacrificial creature," and indicates that the animal in question, the common domestic pig, is the chief animal of Chinese gastronomy and was used widely for Daoist worship and ancestor veneration ceremonies (see the recipe for White Sliced Pork below). On special occasions, large pigs were slaughtered and used for sacrifice by placing them at altars where incense was burned and prayers are made. Following the ceremony, the carcasses were partitioned and given to the worshippers or cooked for a communal celebratory meal. This is still commonly practiced nowadays, and in Taiwan these celebrations are known as *da baibai* 大拜拜 (or great worship ceremony).

Sacrificial Tribe

Pork, Ham, and Meatballs

Pigs are such a widely used culinary animal that they can be considered the "spiritual leaders of the gastronomic realm." The ancients held the pig in especially high regard for the purpose of spiritual offerings and rituals. Assembled here is the List of Sacrificial Animals.

Two Ways of Preparing Pig's Head

Incense sticks (*xiang* 香) were used to measure time in premodern China. Although their duration could vary, based on some of the recipes, we assume that one incense stick burns for about one hour. See also the glossary for more information.

Scrub a five *jin* pig's head clean and add three *jin* of sweet *jiu* to it.[1] If the pig's head is around seven or eight *jin* in weight, use five *jin* of sweet *jiu* instead. Place the pig's head in a pot with the sweet *jiu* and cook it with thirty stalks of green onion and three *qian* of star anise for more than two hundred *gun* [ten minutes]. After that, add one large cup of autumn sauce, one *liang* of sugar, and cook until done. Taste and season with autumn sauce as needed, then add enough boiling water to cover the pig's head by an inch. Weigh the pig's head down with something heavy and boil over high heat for one incense stick worth of time [one hour]. Then reduce the heat and braise using a gentle flame, reducing the liquid according to how rich it is. When the pig's head is tender and soft, immediately remove the lid; otherwise, the fat will be rendered from the flesh.[2]

Another method for preparing pig's head is to first break open [the bottom of] a wooden bucket and install a copper sieve in its center. Wash the pig's head clean, place it in the prepared bucket with the required seasonings, and gently steam everything over the cooking liquid. When the pig's head is cooked and tender, any greasy and foul drippings should have flowed out of the sieved bucket, making the dish exceptionally good.

Four Ways of Preparing Ham Hock

Take a ham hock[3] with the trotter removed and boil it in water until soft. Discard the cooking liquid and add to the meat one *jin* of

---

1 Washing a pig's head is messy business—even more so than the trotters. You have to burn off the bristles, then scrub out all the mucus and dirt located inside and around every nook and cranny of the ears, mouth, gums, eyes, and snout. Some people simplify the overall task by using Coca-Cola instead of water, which does an impressive job due to the phosphoric acid in the drink. The pig's head noted here is quite heavy, and has likely not yet been deboned.

2 This concept was mentioned in the section "Rendering Fat" in the "Objectionables" chapter.

3 The Ham hock refers to the "shin" portion of the pig's hind limbs. Some chefs suggest that the hock has the right quantity of fat and the skin is thin, which makes it good for long braising or

good *jiu*, half a wine cup of light soy sauce, one *qian* of dried tangerine peel, and four or five dried red jujubes, then braise the ham hock until it is soft. When it is done, remove the tangerine peel and red

A wine cup possibly held between thirty and fifty milliliters of fluid.

jujubes, then finish by sprinkling the ham hock with green onions, Sichuan pepper, and *jiu*. This is one method. Another method is to substitute a broth made from simmering dried shrimp in water and to braise the hock in it with *jiu* and autumn sauce.

Hongshao 紅燒, or red cooking, is a cooking technique of braising meat or tofu in dark soy sauce, sugar, and *jiu*.

Yet another method is to boil a ham hock until it is fully cooked, then fry the skin of the hock in vegetable oil until it crisps and turns into crackling. Season and stew the fried ham hock in the manner for red cooking until done. Some scholars like to pull off this crackling and eat the skin first, calling it "lifting off the thin blanket."

Another method involves taking a ham hock and putting it between two earthenware alms bowls together with *jiu* and autumn sauce, and then steaming it separately from the water for a period of two incense sticks [two hours]. This dish is known as Immortal's Pork, which is done excellent at Observer Qian's household.[4]

Trotters and Tendons

Take just the trotters, remove their large bones, and braise them in plain chicken broth. The flavors of the tendons and trotters are similar and match each other

These trotters likely include part of the ham hock (cut high). In Chinese cuisine, it is rare to cook an entire ham together in one dish, in the manner of a western roasted ham.

---

stewing as required in these recipes. Some recipes, however, suggest using the "forearm" portions of the pig's forelimbs, known as the knuckle.

4 Alms bowls are the ceramic bowls that Buddhist monks use for collecting alms. In this description, they are either stacked upside down on top of each other with the ham hock inside, or the hock is put in the smaller bowl, which is placed inside the bigger bowl, like Russian (*matryoshka*) dolls. If the cooking setup was the latter and all the bowls were dry, it would have been a sort of "steam baking" (see also the recipe for Dry-Steamed Pork). If the large bowl had water in it, it would be similar to a bain-marie. The name of the dish, Immortal's Pork, might also come from these alms bowls. Or perhaps the setup of stacking one bowl on top of the other looks like a bottle gourd (or calabash), which is a traditional symbol of Chinese immortals (*shenxian* 神仙, ordinary individuals who transcended the material world) and the mystical medicines they carried in them.

well. If one has a good ham hock with the trotter, it can also be cooked with the tendon.

Two Ways of Preparing Stomach

When braised, pig stomach has a soft, springy texture, which is referred to in Chinese and Taiwanese simply as "Q." The name Q comes from the Southern Min pronunciation of the word *jiu* 粿. It refers to rice that has been pounded in a mortar to a consistency similar to *mochi*.

Wash the stomach and reserve its thickest part. Discard its inner and outer membranes, using only the middle layer. Dice the stomach, stir-fry it in hot oil, season, and then plate it. The crisper the meat's texture, the better it is. This is the northern method of preparation

The southern method involves braising the stomach in a mixture of water and *jiu* for a period of two incense sticks [two hours] until sufficiently soft. It is then dipped in plain salt and eaten. The stomach is also delicious braised with the right seasonings in chicken broth until soft, then smoked and sliced.[5]

Two Ways of Preparing Lung

Lungs are the most difficult to clean of all the organs. First, one has to clear the lungs' bronchi of all traces of blood and remove the membrane surrounding each lung. Then comes the delicate tasks of beating, squeezing, inverting,

Pig lungs were used as a restorative in Chinese medicine for, not surprisingly, the treatment of conditions related to the lungs and the respiratory system.

---

5 Pig stomach has a fantastic crispness when cooked *à point*. The inner membrane (*mucosa*) and the outer membrane (*serosa*) need to be removed before stir-frying due to their tough and unpleasant texture. Only the orthogonal layers of smooth muscle tissues and connective tissue are used. An example of this preparation is the Shandong dish *youbao shuangcui* 油爆雙脆 (two crisp items stir-fried in boiling oil). It consists of rapidly stir-fried chicken gizzards and pig stomach, both cut in a chrysanthemum or lychee-pattern (*lizhi xing* 荔枝型), which is created by deep (but not severing) crisscross cuts, causing the meat to "open up" after cooking, resembling chrysanthemum petals or lychee skin.

and hanging the lung, and pulling out the numerous bronchial branches and tubes.[6]

Prepare the lung by boiling it in a mixture of water and *jiu* for a day and a night. When the lung has shrunk to the size of a white hibiscus blossom, floating on the surface of the liquid, season as required and serve. The lung should be so tender that it falls apart and melts in the mouth.

When the official Tang Xiya hosted banquets, each bowl would be served with four pieces of lung that were originally prepared from four whole lungs. People nowadays no longer have such skill; thus the lungs are prepared by tearing them into small pieces and cooking them in chicken broth until soft, which is still good. This preparation is even better using pheasant broth, which accompanies the gentle flavors of the lung with its own delicate flavors. One can also braise the lung with good ham.

Kidney

If one stir-fries kidney slices until they are well done, they will be as tough and as dry as wood. But serve them tender and they will leave people doubting their doneness. It is preferable to braise the kidneys until soft and eat them dipped in Sichuan pepper salt. Alternately, they can also be finished with one's preferred seasonings.[7]

---

6 The traditional process for cleaning lungs as described by Yuan Mei is messy and tedious. Thanks to modern technology and tools, like kitchen faucets and pressurized water, an innovative "flow-through" lung-cleaning technique has been developed. The pair of lungs is attached directly to the faucet and the lobes of the lungs are punctured with a few jabs of a knife. The water flushes out the blood and mucus via the openings from the punctures. The result is a set of well-cleaned lungs that are snow-white in color and ready for further processing. Some modern recipes don't bother removing the bronchial tubes (the branching, cartilage supported tubes that air into the lung), but instruct to slice them up and then braise.

7 It seems tastes have changed since Yuan Mei's time. These days, kidneys are rarely braised to the point of extreme softness ("soft as mud") as suggested here. Rather, most modern Chinese preparations involve rapid cooking to maintain the crisp texture of the kidneys. A perfect example of this is "stir-fried kidney flowers" (*bao yao hua* 爆腰花), where the clean and prepared kidneys are cut in a lychee or wheat-sheaf pattern (*maisui xing* 麦穗型), parboiled to deodorize them, and rapidly stir-fried in burning hot oil.

To clean the kidneys, pluck out the insides by hand, but do not cut them with a knife.[8] One needs to braise kidneys for a whole day before they are tender and soft as mud. Kidneys should only be cooked on their own and never used with other ingredients, as their off-flavor would overpower everything else. Braise for only three quarters of an hour and kidneys will toughen, but braise them for a day and they become soft and tender.

Tenderloin

Kneading meat with potato, arrowroot, or sweet potato starch is a technique called "velveting." Cornstarch is not suited for this purpose.

Pork tenderloin is finely textured and very tender. Most people, however, do not know how to prepare it.

I had tenderloin at Yangzhou Prefect Xie Yunshan's banquet that was delicious. The meat was sliced, kneaded with starch, then simmered in shrimp broth with shiitake and laver (red algae, genus *Pyropia*, species P. tenera). It must then be immediately removed from the heat when cooked.[9]

White-Sliced Pork

This dish should ideally be prepared using a pig that one raised in their own household. Slaughter the pig and boil it in a large pot until 80 percent cooked. Turn off the heat and let the meat soak in the hot liquid for one *shichen* [two hours] before removing. Cut off the well-exercised meat

A *shichen* 時辰 is a traditional time measurement, equivalent to two hours. Each day was divided into twelve *shichen* units.

from the thighs or shoulders, and serve it thinly sliced. The meat should be neither hot nor cold, but pleasantly warm.

---

8 The white-colored insides of the kidneys, known as the renal pelvis, are where urine filtered from the blood is collected and sent to the bladder. They are likely tough when cooked and potentially stink as well, which justifies their thorough removal.

9 It is unclear whether this dish is served as a soup or if just the tenderloin slices are served.

Northerners are especially adept at the preparation of this dish. Although southerners try their best, they are not quite able to successfully make it. Note that it cannot be made from an assortment of pork cuts purchased from around the market.[10] It is for this reason that when poor scholars[11] have guests over for a banquet, it is better for them to serve bird's nest rather than white-sliced pork, because the latter cannot be served or prepared well in small quantities.

The way to cut the meat for this dish is to slice it using a small sharp knife, mixing the leaner with the fattier slices of meat. The meat can be sliced in any manner desired, be it against the grain or obliquely. As well, broken or torn slices of meat should be served together with everything else, regardless of appearance. In this case, one does opposite of the Sage's admonishment: "Do not eat things that are haphazardly sliced." By serving it this way, one can experience the many types and cuts of meat that can be found in a pig. The Manchurian "ceremonial pork" is the best.[12]

Three Ways of Preparing Red-Cooked Pork

To make red-cooked pork, one can use sweet sauce, autumn sauce, or neither of these two sauces. For each *jin* of meat, add three *qian* of salt, and braise it in *jiu*. If one uses water to cook the pork, it must be boiled away to reduce the cooking liquid. All three methods of preparation produce pork with color as red as amber, thus there is no need to stir-fry sugar in order to color it.[13]

Sweet sauce (*tianjiang* 甜醬) is a sweet, soy-based sauce. It is sometimes used to refer to *tianmian* (sweet dough) sauce.

---

10 This is a very unusual preparation nowadays, when it is usually just one cut of meat boiled in a pot.

11 Although translated here as "poor scholar," the Chinese text literally says "scholars of winter's chill." They are scholars who did not perform well enough in their examinations to gain recognition and state employment. While the term may primarily describe the cold winds these individuals have to endure, it likely also points at their feelings of dejection from their lack of success.

12 This ceremonial pork refers to *tiao shen rou* 跳神肉 (jumping spirit pork), or pigs sacrificed for the Spirit-jumping Ceremony (*tiao shenyi* 跳神儀 or *tiao dashen* 跳大神), a Manchurian shamanic ceremony performed on the first day of the New Year.

13 This describes the process of frying sugar with a small amount of oil in order to make caramel, something that is still commonly done for the preparation of a wide variety of red-cooked meat dishes.

If the meat is removed from the pot too early, it will only be yellowish, but if it is cooked for the right amount of time its color will become an appetizing red. If the pork is cooked or soaked in the cooking liquid for too long, however, the meat will darken from red to purple, and the leaner meats turn dry and hard.[14] Beware: if one continuously opens the lid to check the cooking pork, the oil inside the pork will be rendered out of the meat along with its flavor.

The pork for this dish should be cut into rough cubes and braised until its edges and corners have become round and soft, and the lean meat melts in one's mouth. The success of this dish depends wholly on the strength of the cooking heat. As the proverb goes, "A burning hot flame for congee, but a slow flame for meat." How pertinent a saying indeed!

White-Braised Pork[15]

Boil a *jin* of pork in water until it is 80 percent done. Strain out the liquid, then braise the pork in half a *jin* of *jiu* and two *qian* of salt for one *shichen* [two hours]. After this, pour back half of the liquid used for boiling the pork and reduce it to the desired richness. To finish, add green onions, Sichuan pepper, wood ears, garlic chives, or similar ingredients. When braising meat, the heat must be initially fierce but gentle afterward.

Another method is to first take a *jin* of pork, add one *qian* of sugar, half a *jin* of *jiu*, one *jin* of water, and a half teacup of light soy sauce. Boil the meat first in the *jiu* for ten to twenty *gun* [thirty to

---

14 Some modern recipe books still suggest that the cooking liquid is strained from a red-cooked dish and only added back when serving to prevent the meat from becoming salty, darkened, and hardened.

15 Unlike its well-known red-cooked relative, white-braised pork is rare in modern Chinese cuisine. The closest dish would be the classical preparation of Taiwanese pork hock noodles (*zhujiao mianxian* 猪脚麵線) that used little to no soy sauce. But even this dish now has two variants, "clear-cooked" (*qing dun* 清燉) with salt, and "red-cooked" (*hong shao* 紅燒) with soy sauce. Maybe this reflects a global shift in Chinese cooking, in which darker soy-sauced items are preferred over simpler light flavored dishes. For instance, the term *lu* 滷 was previously used exclusively to describe brine (a solution of salt in water), but it is now commonly used in describing soy-sauce-based braising, for example *lu shui* 滷水 (soy-based stewing liquid) or *lu wei* 滷味 (the items cooked in that stewing liquid).

sixty seconds],[16] then add one *qian* of fennel seeds. Continue simmering the meat until soft, while reducing the cooking liquid to the desire richness. This preparation is also very good.

Fried Pork

Take a slab of pork belly taken from near the ribs and cut it into squares. Remove any sinew and marinate in *jiu* and soy sauce. Fry the pork in a wok with generous amounts of oil until the fat is no longer greasy and the lean meat is tender. To finish the pork, season it with green onions, garlic, and a drizzle of vinegar.

Dry-Steamed Pork

Use a small porcelain bowl. Chop the pork into cubes and combine with sweet *jiu* and autumn sauce, place them in bowl then seal its opening. Place the bowl in the wok to "dry-steam" for a period of two incense sticks [two hours] without any water.

The quantity of autumn sauce and *jiu* to use depends on one's taste and the quantity of meat being prepared. Though, the braising liquids should just cover the top of the meat.

Dry steaming uses several small, thick-walled ceramic bowls placed inside a wok in the manner of a Western-style Dutch oven. The cooking heat is low, slow, even, and perfect for braising. This dish is somewhat akin to a French cassoulet.

Pork in a Lidded Bowl

Prepare the pork as with the previous recipe, but instead place the large bowl directly on top of a hand-warming stove to cook.[17]

---

16 This step is probably used to boil off the alcohol.

17 A hand-warming stove (*shoulu* 手爐) can be either a small portable hand warmer carried by people in their sleeves or just a small stove used at home, often with a handle that would allow carrying it around.

Pork in a Porcelain Urn

Prepare the pork as in the previous recipes, but braise it by placing the covered bowl into smoldering rice chaff. It is important for the lid of the bowl to be tightly sealed in this preparation.[18]

Tuosha Pork

Take a chunk of pork, remove the skin, and chop the meat until it is thoroughly minced. For each *jin* of pork, stir in the yolks and whites of three chicken eggs, then mash the mixture until its texture is fine and smooth. Mix in half a wine cup of autumn sauce and chopped green onion, then wrap this mixture in a large sheet of caul fat. Panfry the wrapped meat in four *liang* of vegetable oil until both sides are done and remove it from the wok.

Unwrap the meat and simmer it gently in one tea cup of good *jiu* and half a wine cup of light soy sauce. Remove it from the wok, slice, and finish with a topping of garlic chives, shiitake mushrooms, and cubes of bamboo shoots.

Tuosha 脫沙 literally means "removing the sand." Jade hunters use it to describe removing the sandy, hazy outer layer from a chunk of raw jade, revealing the precious stone underneath. Removing the crusty fried caul fat from this Chinese-style meatloaf, as described in the second paragraph of the *Tuosha* Pork recipe, has a similar effect. Another interpretation is that *sha* 沙 (sand) may be a shorthand for gauze (*shabu* 紗布), which would refer to the gauzy caul fat that has to be removed before serving. Yet another interpretation is that the *sha* actually refers to a veil (*miansha* 面紗), and thus the name of this dish would be "lifting the veil pork"—a flirtatious name for a humble meatloaf. The method of wrapping ground pork in caul fat is also found throughout Western cuisines. It seems that either different cultures happen upon the same culinary techniques independently, especially if they are on similar latitudes, or that the technique of making meatloaf was transmitted from the West to Qing dynasty China via some trade route.

---

18 Using burning rice chaff is a rare Chinese baking technique, probably taken from farmers who used chaff as cooking fuel. Yuan Mei mentions several dishes that use exotic fuels for cooking. In this recipe, it is critical to seal the container well; otherwise, the pork will end up tasting like smoky rice chaff. The direct application of heat to the bowl may lend this dish a more caramelized flavor than the previous two recipes.

Sun-Dried Pork[19]

Thinly slice some lean pork and lay the slices under strong sunlight until sufficiently dry. Stir-fry the pork with thinly sliced preserved kohlrabi.

Pork Braised with Ham

Cut the dry-cured ham into square pieces and boil them, starting from cold water three times in total, and then drain them dry. Cut the pork into square pieces, then boil them starting from cold water twice and drain them dry.[20] Braise the prepared ham and pork together in water. To finish the dish, add to it four *liang* of *jiu*, green onions, Sichuan pepper, bamboo shoots, and shiitake mushrooms.

Pork Braised with *Taixiang* (Dried Salted Fish from Taizhou)

The technique for this dish is essentially the same as the recipe for "Pork Braised with Ham." Since dried fish softens rapidly when cooked, however, it should be added only when the braising pork is 80 percent done.

When this dish is allowed to cool and gel, it becomes a Shaoxing dish known as "*xiang* aspic."[21] If the dried fish is of bad quality, do not even consider using it.

.

---

19 In modern Chinese cuisine, grilling sun-dried pork or pork jerky before eating it is quite common, but stir-frying pork jerky with other ingredients is uncommon. That said, this dish does sound like an interesting "drinking" snack, accompanying an alcoholic beverage (*xia jiu cai* 下酒菜).

20 Actually, the Chinese phrase translated here as "boil from cold water twice," can have two interpretations. The ham and pork may have been added to cold water, and each time the water boiled, it was discarded and replaced completely with fresh cold water; or the ingredients were added to cold water, and each time the water boiled, the liquid was quenched by adding some cold water before being allowed to come to a boil again. The latter technique is also used to cook water dumplings (*shuijiao* 水饺). Both interpretations would serve to slightly desalt and moisten the dried ham and clean the pork by removing any "gunk" from the surface and congealing any liquid blood still inside it, both of which would cloud up the braising liquid and muddy the taste of the finished dish.

21 This dish is now known in China as *xiang dong rou* 鲞凍肉 or *bai xiang men rou* 白鲞燜肉.

Fenzheng (Steamed) Pork[22]

Tianmian (sweet dough) sauce is sometimes referred to simply as sweet sauce (*tianjiang*). It is a sweet and salty fermented sauce, made from steamed wheat dough, and (occasionally) soybeans.

For this dish, use pork that is half lean and half fatty. First, toast coarsely ground rice until it is golden brown, then mix it together with *tianmian* sauce and the pork. Next, steam the pork in a steaming basket lined with napa cabbage.

When the dish is finished, not only is the pork excellent, the cabbage is also delicious. By not using any water in the dish's preparation, all the flavors are retained within the ingredients. This is a dish from Jiangxi Province.[23]

Smoked Braised Pork

First, braise the pork in autumn sauce and *jiu* until done. Next, smoke the braised pork briefly with its cooking juices over smoldering wood shavings. The pork will be slightly dry on the outside, moist inside, and extremely fragrant and tender. The household of instructor Wu Xiaogu excelled in preparing this dish.

Hibiscus Pork

Slice one *jin* of lean pork, dip each of the slices in light soy sauce, and let them dry in the open air for two hours. Shell forty large shrimps and cut two *liang* of whole lard into small dices. Place one whole shrimp and a piece of lard on each slice

Hibiscus (*furong* 芙蓉) dishes are named so because they are pale in color, with an irregular form and texture, much like the Chinese hibiscus flower. *Furong* dishes typically involve egg, but can also use meat or tofu.

---

22 *Fenzheng* pork (lit. powder steamed pork), although not well-known among Westerners, is a staple dish for many Chinese families and eaten quite often at home. The powder (*fen*) refers to the ground, toasted rice, which is known in modern Chinese cuisine as pork (or meat) steaming powder (*zhu rou fen* 蒸肉粉). It is also used in the *laap* (ลาบ) meat salads of Southeast Asia.

23 Spicy and pickled ingredients feature prominently in Jiangxi cuisine. While this recipe is quite benign, other *fenzheng* pork recipes can be quite spicy or *mala*, a flavor combination from the Sichuan region combining hot and spicy chili peppers with the fragrant numbing flavor of Sichuan pepper.

of pork and pound the shrimp and lard flat onto the pork. Place the pork in boiling water to cook through.

Heat half a *jin* of vegetable oil, place the pieces of pork onto a large skimming spoon, and ladle hot oil over them until done. Bring half a wine cup of autumn sauce, one cup of *jiu*, and half a teacup of chicken broth to boil, and pour on top of the pork. Finish by adding steamed rice noodles, green onions, and Sichuan pepper to the pork before serving.

Lychee Pork[24]

Slice the pork into large domino-like pieces. Boil them in plain water and remove them after twenty to thirty *gun* [sixty to ninety seconds]. Heat half a *jin* of vegetable oil, fry the pork in it until done, then strain. Immediately immerse the pork in cold water to shock it, which will cause the meat to wrinkle up. Strain out the cold pork and cook in half a *jin* of *jiu*, a small cup of soy sauce, and half a *jin* of water until soft.

Eight Treasure Pork

Take one *jin* of pork that is half lean and half fatty. Boil it in plain broth for ten to twenty gun [thirty to sixty seconds], then cut into willow-leaf-shaped pieces. Prepare two *liang* of small mussels, two *liang* of eagle talon shrimp, (*Trachysalambria curvirostris*, cocktail or southern rough shrimp), one *liang* of shiitake, two *liang* of jellyfish, four pieces of walnuts with the membranes removed, four *liang* of bamboo shoot slices, two liang of good dry-cured ham, and one *liang* of sesame oil. Braise the pork in autumn sauce and *jiu* in a pot until half done. Combine the pork with all of the accompanying ingredients and continue braising until done. The jellyfish should be added only at the very end.

---

24 Not only does this recipe not use any lychee, but none of the ingredients could create flavors that even vaguely resemble those of the fruit. Instead, the name of this dish likely refers to the wrinkles on the pork resulting from the special "cold shock" technique, which look like the skin of lychee. It should also be noted that this recipe is very different from that of the modern version of lychee pork, also known as *gulao* or sweet-and-sour pork (*gulao rou* 咕咾肉 or *guilao rou* 鬼老肉). This dish *does* imitate the sweet and sourness of the lychee through the use of vinegar and sugar.

A Note on Eight Treasures

Eight treasure (*babao* 八寶) dishes and beverages are quite typical for celebratory Chinese meals. The eight treasures originally refer to the Buddhist Eight Treasures, attributes or signs that symbolize an enlightened mind, and are often found in temples and in Chinese art. In cuisine, eight treasure dishes range from savory appetizers and main dishes to sweet desserts, but they all contain (roughly) eight different, colorful, flavorful, distinctive, and sometimes expensive ingredients. Usually the base ingredient, such as rice, is not counted as one of the eight treasures. The famous Eight Treasure Rice (*Babao fan* 八寶 飯), for example, is a sweet dish containing eight ingredients (fruit and nuts) in addition to the rice. In the Eight Treasure Pork recipe, however, Yuan Mei does consider the pork precious enough to be counted as one of the "treasures." That said, eight treasure dishes do not necessarily have to include *exactly* eight ingredients. The number eight (*ba* 八) is an auspicious number because it sounds similar to the word for "becoming wealthy" (*fa* 發).

Braised Pork with Cauliflower

Take the tender flower buds of the cauliflower, pickle lightly in brine, and then dry in the sun.[25]

Stir-Fried Pork Strips

Cut the pork into fine strips, remove any sinew, skin, and bones, and then marinate the strips in light soy sauce and *jiu*. Heat a small quantity of vegetable oil in a wok until the white wisps of oil smoke become bluish, then immediately add the strips of pork and stir continuously without pausing. Add steamed rice noodles, a drop of vinegar, and a pinch of sugar. Finish with garlic chives,

---

25 The technique of lightly pickling and drying vegetables and then braising them with meat is similar to the steam-braised pork dish known as *meicai kourou* 梅菜扣肉. It consists of slices of pork stacked at the bottom of a large bowl topped with stir-fried, pickled, and dried mustard leaves (*meigancai* 霉乾菜). The entire bowl is then steamed and inverted onto the serving dish before being brought to the table.

garlic, the white portion of green onions, or similar ingredients. Stir-fry only half a *jin* of the dish at a time at high heat without using any water.[26]

Another method is to fry the pork in oil first then quickly braise it with soy sauce and *jiu*. Plate the pork when it is red in color.[27] The dish is particularly good finished with garlic chives.[28]

Stir-Fried Pork Slices

Use a mixture of half lean and half fatty pork that has been sliced thinly and marinated in soy sauce. Stir-fry the pork in oil. When the pork starts to crackle, add soy sauce, water, green onions, melon,[29] winter bamboo shoots, and yellow garlic chives. Finish the dish by stir-frying over very high heat.

These yellow garlic chives are grown covered with earth to prevent their leaves from turning green and firm, a process known as blanching.

Eight Treasure Meatballs

Take one portion of lean pork and one of fatty pork and mince them into a fine paste. Take pine nuts, shiitake, the tips of bamboo shoots, water chestnuts, soy-pickled cucumbers, and soy-pickled

---

26 This preparation is remarkably similar to the Cantonese stir-fried beef and rice noodle dish *ganchao niuhe* 乾炒牛河. The details about the temperature of the oil, the continuous stirring, and the relatively small portions of ingredients illustrate the key elements of explosive (*bao* 爆) stir-frying. Cooking more pork and using oil that is not burning hot would create a wet, stewed dish devoid of *wokhei* (*huoqi* 鑊氣) flavor.

27 The red color of these "red"-cooked dishes is often exaggerated. In the past, this was done by adding adjectives like "cinnabar crimson," (*zhuhong* 硃紅) and in modern days, food photography enhances the color by tuning the contrast. The color of this dish is actually a dark, reddish brown which comes from the use of soy sauce and occasionally caramelized sugar.

28 Pork strips with garlic chives (*pai cai chao rousi* 韭菜炒肉絲) is a classic Chinese home-style dish (*jiachang cai* 家常菜).

29 The word *gua* 瓜, translated here as melon, is used to describe all manners of "vegetable fruits" under the *Cucurbitaceae* family, including cucumbers, gourds, loofah, watermelons, and squashes. Papaya (*mugua* 木瓜), though not in this phylogenetic group, is also considered a *gua* due to its shape. The edible varieties of the bottle gourd (*hugua* 瓠瓜), including cucumber (*huanggua* 黃瓜) and the miniature winter melon (*maogua* 毛瓜) (*Benincasa hispida var. chieh-qua*) would all work well for this recipe.

ginger, then mince them into a fine paste as well. Combine everything with powdered starch and shape the mixture into balls. Place the meatballs on a dish and steam with sweet *jiu* and autumn sauce. When eaten, the texture of the meatballs should be crisp and tender. Jia Zhihua once said, "To make meatballs, the meat should be finely cut and not chopped."[30] There is truth in his statement.

Hollow Meatballs

Pound the pork until it becomes a thick paste. Roll cold rendered lard into balls, then use them to fill each pounded pork meatball. Steam the filled meatballs so that the fat melts and flows away, leaving each meatball with a hollow core. The people of Zhenjiang are especially good at preparing this dish.[31]

"Wok-Roasted" Pork[32]

Boil the pork with its skin on until done, then pan-fry it with sesame oil in the wok. Cut the pork into pieces and serve with salt. Alternatively, the pork can be eaten dipped in light soy sauce.

---

30 Finely cut, rather than chopped, pork produces a more evenly sized mince. This in turn produces meatballs with a more consistent and enjoyable texture. Even particle size is of great matter in cuisine: even if they cannot be easily noticed, the results are immediately perceivable. For instance, coffee beans ground using a mill rather than a blade grinder are much cleaner and less bitter in taste, since the grinds are more even with less deviations in their size distribution. This allow elution times from the grinds to be precisely set so the best flavours are extracted from the grinds while leaving more of the unpleasant flavors behind.

31 This is a gimmicky dish created for the sole purpose of impressing and eliciting praise from one's guests.

32 Roasted (or broiled) pork (*shaorou* 燒肉) involves roasting the whole animal and is almost always prepared using custom-built ovens. This ensures that the pork skin turns into crisp crackling while the meat remains juicy and tender. Yuan Mei's wok-roasted pork allows one to cook smaller portions of pork while still achieving the same-textured skin and meat. Actually, the "roasting" part of the dish's name is a bit of a misnomer, since the technique is actually boiling and pan-frying pork. That said, *shao* is on occasion used to refer to cooking in general (e.g., *shao cai* 燒菜 means cooking dishes, not roasting them). Nevertheless, boiling in water would have kept the meat moist, and frying in sesame oil would have turned the skin into fragrant golden-brown crackling.

Marinated Pork

Lightly cure the pork with salt, then marinate in *tianmian* sauce. Alternatively, mix the pork well with autumn sauce. Let it dry in the wind.

Lees Pork

Lightly marinate the pork with salt, and then add rice wine lees to it.[33]

Marinated pork (*jiangrou* 醬肉) is a cured and dried meat product, similar to what is known today as *larou* 臘肉 , or dry-cured pork. *Larou* is made during the twelfth month of the Chinese lunar year, called *layue*, hence the name.

Lightly Salted Pork[34]

Rub and knead a piece of pork with a small amount of salt and let it cure. Use it within three days' time. Note these previous three dishes are for the winter months. They are not suitable for spring and summer.[35]

The Wind-Dried Pork of Master Yin Wenduan's Household[36]

Slaughter a pig and portion the carcass into eight pieces. Stir-fry four *qian* of salt for each piece of pork and meticulously rub

---

33 The process of marinating the pork in salt and wine lees probably took about one full day. The brevity of this recipe indicates that preparing lees pork was something everybody knew how to do back then.

34 *Baoyan* 暴醃 literally translates as "exposed salt." The term itself comes from a northern Chinese local dialect and describes a salting technique that is used to prepare napa cabbage for making the Chinese equivalent of kimchi. Salt is rubbed on the food item, which is then allowed to rest in a cool place while its surface dries slightly and excess water is pulled out by the salt. The cooking method for *baoyan* pork may be similar to lightly salted fish (*baoyan yu* 暴醃魚), which involves pan-frying and braising.

35 The last three recipes consist of lightly salted raw pork that needs the cold winter weather to prevent it from spoilage and insect infestation. Although less likely, these could also be a technique for curing meat that is too excessively heating (*shu* 暑) to the body during hot seasons, according to Traditional Chinese Medicine.

36 Wind-drying describes the method of dry-curing pork by exposing it to cool wind. Although this is a pretty typical way of making cured pork (or other meats) in Chinese cuisine, what is interesting about this recipe is that it uses *all* the parts of the pig, not just the more popular ham and belly.

the pork with the salt such that not a speck of the surface is left unsalted. Next, hang the salted pork pieces high in a windy but shaded location. If, by chance, one finds insects or maggots chewing on parts of the pork, simply apply sesame oil to these parts.[37]

Wind-dried pork is best eaten during summer. To prepare, first soak the pork overnight in water before cooking. Note that one should not use too little or too much water when cooking. Rather, use just enough to cover the piece of pork. When cutting, use a sharp knife to shave the pork into thin slices against the grain of the meat.

The Yin household makes this item so well that it is often sent as an Imperial tribute item. Even the wind-dried pork of present-day Xuzhou cannot compare with it. As for how they make it so well, no one knows.[38]

Home-Style Pork[39]

There are important differences in the quality of home-style pork from Hangzhou. They can be grouped into three different grades: high, medium, and low. High-grade items should be mildly salty but still exhibit umami, with lean meat that is tender enough to bite into. When these high-quality specimens of home-cured pork are aged, they become excellent dried hams.

---

37 This use of sesame oil is not very common, and why exactly it is used remains unclear, perhaps preventing those spots from drying out, or acting as an insect repellent. The possibility of insect infestation hints at the fact that wind-dried pork can be made in early winter or late autumn, when the weather is warmer and insects are more prevalent.

38 This sounds like *terroir*: the way the pig was raised, the coolness and humidity of the location, and native wind that dried the pork. It could also very well be the skill of the person making it, or a combination of those things.

39 While many Chinese communities make dry-cured pork, Zhejiang Province is so well-known for this product that even today cities like Jinhua (neighboring Hangzhou) are inextricably linked to cured pork. This home-style pork recipe indeed refers to none other than the internationally acclaimed Jinhua ham.

Braised Ham with Bamboo Shoots

Slice winter bamboo shoots and the dry-cured ham into square pieces and braise them together. Soak the ham twice in water to rid it of salt, then add rock sugar and braise until soft.[40]

Official Xi Wushan indicated that if one has already braised the ham but wishes to save it for a meal the following day, it is important that it be kept immersed in its braising liquid.[41] Come the next day, simmer the ham in the liquid just until it is hot enough to be served. Should the ham be stored dry without its braising liquid, it will toughen and desiccate. On the other hand, keeping the ham immersed in water would make it flavorless.

Roasted Suckling Pig

Take a suckling pig weighing six to seven *jin*, pull out any hairs, and scrub it clean of blood and filth. Skewer the pig and roast it on top of a charcoal fire. All sides of the pig must be evenly roasted until its skin is dark golden brown in color. Slowly and continuously baste the skin with butter while roasting.

Roasted suckling pigs with delicately crisp skin are considered the best, those with crunchy skin are of lesser quality, while those with hard tough skin are ranked the worst. The Manchu have a method of making suckling pig by steaming it with *jiu* and autumn sauce. In my family, it is my younger brother [Yuan] Longwen who has mastered this method of preparation.

---

40 If one were to follow the instructions exactly, one would braise the bamboo shoots with the ham, and then wash the ham in cold water twice, essentially throwing away all flavor. Alternatively, just braising the ham with the bamboo shoots all the way with sugar would make this dish overly salty. It is therefore likely that the order of this recipe should be as follows: First, soak the block of ham twice with fresh changes of water. Second, cut both the ham and bamboo shoots into squares. Finally, braise all ingredients with rock sugar.

41 This method of storing should probably only be used with ham. Red-cooked meats should be kept separately from their cooking liquid, if prolonged storage is required, so that they do not become tough and overly salty. The two should be recombined only when the dish needs to be reheated before serving. In fact, this is the method recommended by Jesse Lee 李嘉茜 in her simple but excellent cookbook *Shanghai Flavors* 上海味兒.

Roasted Pork

Roasting a whole pig requires, above all, patience. The interior of the pig should be roasted first so the pork's fat is infused into the skin, making it tender, crisp, and full of flavor. If one should start by roasting the skin first, however, the fat between it and the meat will melt away and drip into the flames, producing roasted pork with skin that is charred and tough with poor flavor. This same technique applies when roasting suckling pigs.[42]

Ribs

Take sliced pork ribs with meat that is half lean and half fatty. Pull out the rib bones from the meat and stuff the cavities with stalks of green onions.[43] Grill the ribs while constantly brushing with vinegar and soy sauce. Do not let the ribs be grilled too dry.

Luosuo Pork

Prepare this dish as one would the recipe for minced chicken.[44] Reserve the piece of skin on the pork for use as a cover, and chop

---

42 Though the techniques may be somewhat similar, roasted pork is much more difficult to make than roasted suckling pig, because of the stronger flavor and firmer meat of the older animal. When the ingredients consist of just a whole pig with some salt and oil, any fault in technique and preparation is laid bare to the diner.

43 This recipe appears to be missing a few steps. Pulling the bones out of a raw or just-cooked rack of ribs is close to impossible. Even if you could do so, grilling the ribs starting from its raw state would result in incredibly tough ribs. For this recipe to work, the pork ribs must first be stewed or steamed until somewhat tender. From there, the rib bones can be twisted and pulled out, and the meat stuffed with stalks of green onions and grilled, as specified in the recipe.

44 The recipe for minced chicken (*ji song* 雞鬆) is found in the "Winged Tribe" chapter. Minced dishes consist of finely chopped ingredients that are served on top of rice, wrapped in pancakes, or cradled in iceberg lettuce. An example is minced duck (*ya song* 鴨鬆), which is served as the second dish (after the duck skin) when eating Peking duck in the "one duck, three dishes" (*yi ya san chi* 一鴨三吃) form. Eventhough this recipe is similar in prepration to the other minced dishes, it is not called *rou song* 肉鬆 because that name is already used for what is translated in English as "pork floss". Floss dishes, like the fish floss dish found in the "Water Tribe" chapter, are made of made of stir-fried, mashed, and dried meat. Thus, the word *song* 鬆 can be translated as both "minced" and "floss." The only way of correctly identifying the dish at hand is by looking at the context and instructions.

the lean meat taken from under it into a coarse mince.[45] Season the minced pork and cook. This dish is a specialty of chef Nie Xu.

Three Pork Dishes from Duanzhou

The first is *luosuo* pork. The second is plain boiled pork tossed with sesame seeds and salt. The last is sliced and braised pork tossed with light soy sauce. These three dishes are great for home cooking.

Chef Nie and chef Li of Duanzhou excel at making these three dishes, so much so that I asked [my chef] Yang'er to go to the chefs in order to learn the dishes' preparation.[46]

Prefect Yang Meatballs

The meatballs made by Prefect Yang are as large as teacups and are unsurpassed in delicateness and flavor. Served in a clear umami-flavored soup, these meatballs melt in the mouth. They are likely made from a mixture of half lean and half fatty pork with tendons and ligaments removed, minced finely and held together with starch.[47]

---

45 Essentially the pork skin is removed, reserved, and used as a lid to cover the chopped and seasoned pork as it cooks, exactly in the same manner as the chicken skin is used for minced chicken in that recipe.

46 Considering the simplicity of the three dishes, the chefs must truly have been masters to make such an impression on Yuan Mei as to send his own chef more than a thousand kilometers away to a district in Guangzhou (Canton) to learn how to prepare them.

47 Using starch is like using salt: one must use the minimal amount necessary or risk ruining a dish. An alternative technique comes from Liang Shiqiu's 梁實秋 food memoir *Yashe Discusses Cuisines* 雅舍談吃 (1985), where starch was actually not used in the ground meat mixture itself. Only after the meatball has been shaped does one rub a small amount of starch onto its surface. Meatballs made using this method hold their form, are light and tender, and, most importantly, still taste like meat.

Ham Braised with Napa Cabbage Hearts[48]

Take a good ham and peel off its skin, remove the fat, and reserve the meat. First braise the skin in chicken broth until tender, then add the meat of the ham and braise it until tender. Cut the napa cabbage hearts with the stem into two-inch-long pieces. Add the cabbage along with honey and fresh rice *jiu* to the ham, then braise for half a day.

In Chinese cuisines, braising is the preferred method for cooking napa cabbage (*Brassica rapa* subsp. *pekinensis*), using only the sweet-tasting, bright-yellow, endive-shaped heart. Unlike the European cabbage (*Brassica oleracea var. capitata*), which starts to smell if overcooked, napa cabbage becomes sweeter and more delicious the longer it is braised.

The flavors of this dish are sweet and savory. While the meat and vegetables are very soft, the stem and leaves of the cabbage nevertheless hold their form. The flavors of the broth are incredible. This recipe comes from the head Daoist at Chaotian Temple.

Honeyed Ham

Chop a good ham into large chunks with the skin-on, and braise that in sweet *jiu* until they are soft and tender. This is an excellent dish.

Note though, the differences between a good and bad ham are as great as the distances between the heavens and the abyss. There are numerous well-known hams from the cities of Jinhua, Lanxi, and Yiwu that simply do not live up to their reputations. These bad hams are frankly no better than dried salted pork.

---

48 A half day of braising as is mentioned in this recipe seems excessive, since a good forty minutes would be more than enough to completely soften the napa hearts.

Wangsan's store in Zhongqingli (Hangzhou) sells a very good ham that costs four *qian* coins[49] per *jin*. I have had this ham once at the household of Master Yin Wenduan. Its fragrance was so intense that the neighbors could smell it during preparation, and its flavors were uncommonly good. Sadly, I have never had such an extraordinary ham since.

---

49 The quantity *qian* 錢 was used in China's later dynasties to denote a unit of weight as well to refer to currency. Not surprisingly, the two are related, in that one thousand *qian* is equal to one *liang* in weight, while one thousand *wen* 文 of coins (commonly called *qian*) converts to one *liang* of pure silver. The weight of a *wen* coin also hovered around one *qian*, with the actual quantity depending on the availability of copper. In this text, Yuan Mei uses *qian* to refer to the unit of currency—four coins for one *jin* of ham.

A Note on Livestock

While venison is still not commonly found on Chinese menus, beef and mutton have become staple meats, almost like pork or chicken. Still, mutton retains an air of exoticism in Chinese cuisine because it is generally associated with Chinese minorities of Central Asian and Mongolian ethnic backgrounds. This is also reflected by the generous use of spices, such as the ubiquitous chili pepper and cumin, and the preparation—usually grilling and roasting. In Chinese, the term *yang* can actually refer to sheep, lamb, or even goat. Beef, though omnipresent in modern Chinese cuisine, is still seen as less "morally wholesome," especially in Taiwan and parts of southern China.

Hoofed Tribe

Assorted Lifestock: Beef, Mutton, and Deer

Cattle, sheep, and deer are three animals that are not commonly served in the households of southerners. One cannot, however, be ignorant of their preparations, thus I compiled a list of assorted livestock recipes.

Beef

The way to purchase beef is as follows: one must go to all the butchers on the market and put down enough money to reserve that cut of meat sandwiched between the back legs' tendons that is neither too lean nor too fat.[1] Bring this cut home and slice off any sinew or membranes, then take three parts *jiu* and two parts water to braise it until soft. Reduce the cooking liquid and add autumn sauce.

Note that beef has a unique and distinct flavor that should not be accompanied with other ingredients.

Beef Tongue

Beef tongue is one of the best foods around. Remove the tough skin, shave off the membrane, slice it, and cook it together with braised beef.[2]

It can also be salted and air-dried in the winter for eating the following year.[3] When prepared thus, it has all the qualities of an excellent ham.

Sheep's Head

The hair on the sheep's head must be completely removed; any hair that cannot be removed should be burned off with a flame. Wash the head clean, cut it open, boil it in water until soft, and remove the bones. The old coarse skin inside the sheep's mouth must be thoroughly cleaned. Slice the eyes into two, remove the dark retina and the lens, then chop the eyes into a fine dice.

---

1 While Yuan Mei highly regards this cut of beef from the leg, Western cuisine tends to view it with indifference. This demonstrates cultural preferences in animal portions and cuts. For instance, beef and pork tendons sell at a higher price in East Asia because of their scarcity, and fish heads and skin are eaten as a delicacy. In Western cuisine, these parts are discarded, rendered into by-products, or ground up and turned into meat fillers.

2 Note that in preparing beef tongue, one first has to boil it in order to remove the tough and spiky outer skin. If this isn't done, skinning the tongue would be very difficult. Braising different cuts of meat from the same animal together improves the flavor and texture, and in this case, the beef tongue would get a bolder and beefier flavor. This is also a well-known strategy in Taiwan for making beef noodles (*niurou mian* 牛肉麵).

3 This is a rather uncommon cured meat recipe in modern Chinese cuisine.

Simmer the head in the broth made from a fat old hen along with shiitake mushrooms, diced bamboo shoots, four *liang* of sweet *jiu*, and one cup of autumn sauce. If one desires a spicier dish, add twelve peppercorns and twelve stalks of green onion flowers into the cooking liquid. If one desires a sourer dish, add a cup of good rice vinegar.[4]

Mutton Shank

Mutton shanks can be braised similarly to pork knuckles in either the red-cooked or white-cooked forms. In general, that which is cooked in light soy sauce is red-cooked, and that cooked with salt is white-cooked. The shanks are very good served with mountain yam.

Mutton Soup[5]

Take some cooked mutton and cut it into small pieces, about the size of dice. Braise the meat in chicken broth. Add diced bamboo shoots, diced shiitake mushrooms, diced mountain yam, and then braise until done.

Sheep's Stomach Soup

Wash the sheep's stomach clean, boil until soft, slice into thin strips, and braise in its boiling liquid. Pepper and vinegar can be added when braising the stomach. The northerners have a technique for making stir-fried sheep's stomach, but southerners that prepare it fail to get the desired crisp texture.[6] Prefect Qian Yusha

---

4 The latter two variations are probably also effective at curbing the smellyness or stench of the sheep's head.

5 Mutton *soup* is rarely called *yang geng* 羊羹 nowadays, but rather *yangrou geng* 羊肉羹 (lit. sheep-meat *geng*). The addition of *rou* 肉 is required because *yang geng* alone usually refers to Japanese *yōkan*, a sugary bean jelly that is largely unrelated to mutton *geng* except for its culinary ancestry: a mutton *geng* made with gelatinous broth that becomes an aspic when chilled. Medieval Chinese vegetarian Buddhists who moved from China to Japan replaced the meat with bean paste and starch. The Japanese then replaced the starch with agar and added sugar into the mix, turning it into a sweet dish. This was how *yang geng* went from a savory meaty soup to a sweet, sugary block of firm bean jelly.

6 From these sentences, it becomes clear that Yuan Mei is implying that braising the stomach was the southern Chinese preparation, since northerners prefer it crisp. The fact that the sheep

makes a very good pan-fried mutton. I will soon learn how to prepare it from him.[7]

Red-Cooked Mutton

The preparation of this dish is similar to red-cooked pork. Add shelled walnuts[8] while braising to cut the mutton's strong odor. This is an old technique.

Stir-Fried Mutton Strips

The preparation of this dish is similar to stir-fried pork strips. One can add starch to the meat. The more thinly cut the meat is, the better. Mix slivered green onion into the mutton when done.

Flame-Broiled Mutton

Cut a large five to seven *jin* chunk of mutton into large pieces, and skewer them on iron skewers to broil over flames. The mutton's flavors are delectably sweet, and the texture crisp. It is no wonder the thought of it caused Emperor Renzong of the Song dynasty such cravings in middle of the night.

Whole Sheep

There are seventy-two techniques for preparing the whole sheep,[9] but of all these different preparations, there are only about

---

stomach is prepared similarly to the southern Chinese pork stomach recipe mentioned in the previous chapter is also a good indication that it is a southern style.

7 Yuan Mei did not actually write up a recipe for pan-fried mutton in this book. What exactly the relationship is between this pan-fried mutton and the sheep stomach remains unclear.

8 It is possible that the walnuts specified here were actually young green walnuts that were pierced with a needle and cooked whole with their fleshy outer part. Pierced green walnuts in both fresh and pickled form are found in traditional European cuisines, but are very uncommon in Chinese cuisine.

9 The number seventy-two is used here to indicate "many" or "numerous." It directly refers to the "seventy-two transformations" of the polymorphic Monkey King (Sun Wukong), a character from the famous Ming dynasty novel *Journey to the West*.

eighteen or nineteen that can be considered edible. Much like slaying dragons, the skills for preparing whole sheep are quite esoteric;[10] as such, it is difficult for a home chef to master. When the whole sheep is served in a large dish or a bowl, one should be able to enjoy the distinct flavors of all cuts of meat from the animal; only then can the dish be considered a success.[11]

Venison[12]

Venison is hard to procure. Once acquired and prepared, it is more tender, delicate, and sweeter than the meat of the water deer. It can be prepared grilled or braised.

Two Ways of Preparing Deer Tendon

Deer tendon does not soften easily. For the first three days of preparations, one must pound and boil the tendons numerous times, while continually wringing out any foul-smelling juices from within it. Next, braise the deer tendon in pork broth and then, after that, braise it in chicken broth. Add autumn sauce, *jiu*, and starch to thicken and reduce the cooking liquid.

The tendon can be served as a white-cooked dish without addition of anything else. They can also be braised together with ham, winter bamboo shoots, and shiitake until they take on a reddish hue, and then served in a bowl without reduction. To finish the white-cooked dish, sprinkle it with finely ground Sichuan pepper.

---

10 The idiom "skills for slaying dragons" (*tu long zhi ji* 屠龍之技) is used to describe a highly refined and specialized skill that requires a lot of experience and training.

11 This is most likely a "meal for the eyes," as Yuan Mei would put it. Since each cut of meat, each muscle group, requires vastly different cooking techniques, cooking a whole animal successfully is a very difficult task. Even if done well, the result might not rival a well-cooked mutton dish with a specific cut of meat.

12 Although he doesn't specify, Yuan Mei's venison likely comes from the sika deer (*meihua lu* 梅花鹿). These deer are quite common in the wild throughout China and they have a historical connection to hunting and medicine, and by extension likely also to cuisine.

Water Deer

Prepare meat from the water deer as one would from beef or venison. It can also be dried into jerky. Water deer meat is not as tender and succulent as venison, but it is much finer and smoother in texture.

Native to China and Korea, the water dear (*Hydropotes inermis*) is somewhat similar to the appearance of the musk deer, due to the fang-like tusks protruding from its mouth.

Masked Palm Civet

The masked palm civet (*Paguma larvata*) is native to India and Southeast Asia.

It is hard to find masked palm civet in fresh form. To prepare dry-cured civet, steam it with sweet wine lees until done, and serve it cut into slices with a sharp knife. Be sure to soak dry-cured civet in rice water for a full day to remove excess salt from the meat. Civet is more tender and oilier than a dry-cured ham.

Imitation Milk[13]

Take egg whites and mix them with honey and wine lees. Beat the mixture until even, then steam it. Cook until the mixture has set but is still tender. Do not overcook or else it will become tough. Likewise, using too many egg whites will make the dish tough.

Deer Tail

Master Yin Wenduan ranks deer tail number one among all foods. Deer tail, however, is not readily available to southerners, and those brought in from Beijing are bitter and stale. I once got an especially large specimen and steamed it wrapped in vegetable leaves. It tasted great. The best part of the tail is on top, with a thick layer of fat just under the skin.

Deer tail comes from the far north of China, and is eaten as much for tonic and medicinal reasons as for its exotic appeal.

---

13 Yuan Mei's imitation milk shows that contemporary dishes such as stir-fried (*chao xian nai* 炒鲜奶) or double-skinned "milk" (*shuang nai pi* 雙奶皮), which are essentially pan-cooked or steamed egg-white custards, have had a rather long history in Chinese cuisine.

A Note on Birds

This chapter contains a wide variety of bird recipes, mainly chicken, duck, and other domesticated birds. The translation "Winged Tribe" follows Yuan Mei's somewhat cryptic title *yuzu* 羽族 for poetic and stylistic reasons.

Winged Tribe

Birds: Chicken and Poultry

Chicken plays a substantial role in cuisine, and the success of most recipes is utterly dependent on it. The effect is similar to a virtuous person, who performs good deeds without the knowledge of others. For this reason, we will start with chicken and leave the other birds and poultry for the end. The following is a collection of winged tribe recipes.

White-Cut Chicken

Good white-cut chicken embodies the pure flavors of the unadulterated stocks and extracts used by the ancients.[1] Order this simple dish when one happens to dine at a village inn too busy to cook more involved dishes. When preparing this dish, do not use too much water.

Minced Chicken

Take the legs of a plump chicken, remove their tendons and bones, then mince the meat finely. Be sure not to damage the skin. Mix the meat together with egg whites, starch thickening, and chopped pine nuts. If there is not enough leg meat, substitute with some cubed chicken breast meat.

Fry the meat in sesame oil until golden brown and place it in an earthenware crock. To the crock, add half a *jin* of *baihua* liquor, a large cup of autumn sauce, [and] a ladle of chicken fat, along with the likes of winter bamboo shoots, shiitake, ginger, and green onions. Cover the mixture with the reserved chicken skin,[2] add a large bowl of water, and steam it until done. Remove the chicken skin when serving.[3]

Raw Stir-Fried Chicken

Take a young chicken, chop it into square pieces, and mix with a marinade of autumn sauce and rice *jiu*. When the diners are ready

---

1 Despite its simplicity, white-sliced chicken is indeed a food of surprising profundity. One could say it is a gustatory version of the rock garden, a meditation aid to help put things into perspective and reveal what is hidden in plain sight. Eating it, one begins to understand what the best cuisines can do for people: gently nourish their bodies, comfort their souls, and bring delight to their lives.

2 It is curious why one would cover the bowl with a piece of skin rather than a normal lid. Maybe it gives the meat special flavors, a more pleasant texture, or it somehow regulates the cooking moisture in the way that some chefs use parchment paper as a lid when braising meat (see, for example, Thomas Keller's *The French Laundry Cookbook*). By looking at how minced chicken is steamed while covered with its own skin, based on the instructions there, we can surmise that the same was done for the recipe for *luosuo* pork mentioned in the "Sacrificial Tribe" chapter.

3 In modern Chinese cooking, this dish is usually stir-fried without the extra step of steaming, giving it a more assertive flavor.

for the chicken, take the pieces out of the marinade and sear them in a pan of boiling-hot oil. Remove the chicken from the pan, and repeat this searing process three times in a row.[4] Sprinkle vinegar, rice *jiu*, starch thickening, and chopped green onion on the chicken immediately before plating.

Raw stir-frying (*shengchao* 生炒, *shengbao* 生爆) is special, because in Chinese cooking, it is more common to parcook or deep-fry an ingredient before stir-frying. This speeds up the stir-frying process and ensures even cooking.

Chicken Congee[5]

Take a fat hen, skin and cut off both breasts, then use the knife and scrape the breast meat into a fine paste.[6] One can also use a planing knife for this task. Only scrape and do not chop the meat since the desired fine texture cannot be achieved by chopping. Use the rest of the chicken to make the broth for cooking the scraped meat. When one is ready to serve the dish, pound together a mixture of ground rice flour, minced dried-cured ham, and pine nuts, and add the mixture to the cooking soup. Finish by adding green onions, ginger, and a drizzle of chicken fat.

The soup can either be skimmed of the froth from its surface or left as is, if preferred. It is well suited for serving to the elderly. In general, if the breast meat was chopped for preparation of this soup, then the froth should be skimmed. If the meat was scraped, however, then no skimming is required.

---

4 This repeated sear-and-remove technique is not very common in modern Chinese cuisines. It is likely to prevent the accumulation of juices seeping from the chicken in the wok, keeping it hot enough to give the chicken the right texture and good *wokhei*.

5 This is essentially a soup made with scraped chicken, but because of the paste and the addition of rice flour, the soup has a texture similar to rice congee.

6 Scraping meat or flesh is commonly used in preparing fish balls, dumpling fillings, and other foods requiring fine-textured meat. It is also used in the decadent *jin tang* 吊湯, an intensely flavored broth made by clarifying chicken broth using the scraped breast meat of another chicken. If well made, the broth is clear and almost colorless, with an intense chicken flavor.

Browned Chicken

Wash a fat hen clean and boil it whole in a pot. Add two *liang* of lard and four fennel seeds[7] to the chicken and cook until it is around 80 percent done. Next, take out the chicken and sear in sesame oil until golden brown, then put it back into the liquid to cook.[8] Simmer until the cooking liquid has thickened, then add autumn sauce, *jiu*, and a whole stalk of green onions, and simmer to reduce the liquid to a glaze. When one is about to serve the chicken, chop it into slices, and ladle the glaze on the chicken. One can also toss the chicken in the glaze or serve it on the side as a dip. This is a recipe from the household of Yang Zhongcheng, but the one from Brother Fangfu's household is also good.

Pounded Chicken

Pound a whole chicken until the bones are broken and then cook it in autumn sauce and *jiu*.[9] The household of Nanjing Prefect Gao Nanchang prepares this dish exceptionally well.

Stir-Fried Chicken Slices

Take boneless chicken breasts and chop them into thin slices. Mix the slices with mung bean starch,[10] sesame oil, and autumn sauce. Next add thickening starch and mix in egg whites. Just before stir-frying, add to it soy sauce, soy-pickled cucumbers, soy-pickled ginger, and chopped green onion. One must use a burning-hot flame to stir-fry the dish. Only four *liang* of chicken should be used per serving so that the heat can properly and rapidly cook the meat.

---

7 Four fennel seeds seem very few. Perhaps the measure was left out in the Chinese.

8 When cooking soy sauce duck, browning it before braising is standard. Yuan Mei's method, however, does the browning when the chicken is almost done, which is less common. It probably changes the texture of the skin.

9 Pounding a chicken and breaking its bones probably tenderizes the meat and releases the bone marrow to flavor the chicken as it cooks.

10 The Chinese word *doufen*, translated here as "mung bean starch," literally means "bean flour." It could also refer to mung bean flour, roasted soybean powder, or raw soybean powder.

Steamed Young Chicken[11]

Place a whole tender young chicken on a plate. Add autumn sauce, sweet *jiu*, shiitake mushrooms, and bamboo shoots to it, then steam everything over a rice pot.

Chicken Marinated in Soy Sauce

Take a raw chicken, brine it in soy sauce for a day and a night, then hang it in the breeze to dry.[12] This is a dish for the depth of winter.[13]

Diced Chicken

Take some chicken breasts, cut them into a small dice, and stir-fry them in boiling hot oil. Add autumn sauce and *jiu* to the chicken and remove from the pan. Toss the chicken with diced water chestnuts, dice bamboo shoot tips, and diced shiitake; the ones producing a dark broth being the best.[14]

Chicken Meatballs

This dish consists of minced chicken-breast meat formed into balls as large as wine cups. They are savory and tender like shrimp balls. The household of Yangzhou Magistrate Zangba prepares this dish

---

11 The chicken used in this recipe is probably an older chick, about a month or two old, similar in texture and size to the "game hen" today.

12 This recipe is reminiscent of *fengji* 風雞 (wind chicken), which is first marinated in salt and *jiu*, and then left to dry in the wind. Yuan Mei did not give any instructions on how to cook it after it is dried, but, given that air-dried meats are typically prepared by steaming, that is probably also the way to cook this marinated chicken.

13 The depth of winter (*san dong* 三冬, lit. three winters) refers to the last three months of the lunar calendar, around November, December, and January.

14 The reference to "dark broth" appears out of nowhere. Since all the other ingredients are light-colored, one can only assume that Yuan Mei was referring to the shiitake, which, when soaked from its dry form or cooked in soup, lends a clear, darkish-tan broth. It is also possible that Yuan Mei refers to the entire dish, preferring one that exudes dark juices, but this is the less likely interpretation.

extremely well. The meat is kneaded into balls with pork fat, radish, and starch.[15] They must not be stuffed with fillings.

Chicken Braised with Mushrooms[16]

White button mushrooms (*Agaricus bisporus*) were a common ingredient in mid-Qing cuisine. The Chinese name (*kou mogu* 口蘑菇) means "mouth mushrooms," possibly due to the fact that the younger specimens are perfectly round and bite-size.

Take four *liang* of white button mushrooms, soak them in boiling water to rid them of sand, then swirl them in a bath of cold water. Clean the mushrooms well with a toothbrush,[17] then bathe them in four changes of clean water. Stir-fry the mushrooms over high heat in two *liang* of vegetable oil until done, then dress them with several sprays of *jiu*.

Chop the chicken into square pieces and boil them in a pot. Skim off the floating foam, add sweet *jiu* and light soy sauce, then braise the chicken for 80 percent of the total required time. Add the mushrooms to the chicken and braise everything for the remaining twenty percent of time. Add bamboo shoots, green onions, and Sichuan pepper, and serve. Do not add water when preparing the dish. Garnish with three *qian* of rock sugar. [18]

Chicken Stir-Fried with Pear

Take chicken breasts from a young bird and slice them. Heat up three *liang* of rendered lard and stir-fry the chicken, giving it three or four tosses. Add a large spoon of sesame oil, and a small spoon each

Small spoons (*chachi* 茶匙, lit. teaspoon) were small scoops (*shao* 勺) used for cleaning teapots in tea ceremonies. They probably had the size of half a modern teaspoon.

---

15 This is similar to how shrimp cakes are made (pan-fried) and eaten (straight up). While it is possible to cook them in a soup, this is probably not the best technique, as prolonged cooking tends to make breast meat floury and dry.

16 This recipe is repeated, in a less complete form, later in this chapter (see "Braised Chicken with Mushrooms"). It appears that the manuscript was not carefully edited.

17 Bristle toothbrushes were already in use in China by the fifteenth century. They were made from coarse hog hairs that were attached to bone or bamboo handles.

18 Finishing a dish with *rock* sugar and in such large quantities (around twelve grams) was unusual. Given the cost of sugar back then, this may have been a display of wealth.

of powdered starch, fine salt, ginger juice, and Sichuan pepper. Finally, add finely sliced snow pear[19] and small pieces of shiitake, then stir-fry everything for three or four tosses before plating it in a five-inch dish.

Imitation Pheasant Rolls[20]

Take a chicken breast, chop the meat finely, mix in a chicken egg, and season it with enough light soy sauce to make it fragrant. Take a large piece of caul fat and cut it into squares. Wrap the mixture into small rolls with the cut squares of caul fat and fry them until they are fully cooked. Finish by stir-frying the rolls with light soy sauce, *jiu*, shiitake, and wood ear mushrooms. Throw on a pinch of sugar after plating.

Chicken Stir-Fried with Napa Cabbage

Cut the chicken into pieces, and heat up a wok and stir-fry them until they're no longer raw. Add *jiu* to the chicken and boil twenty to thirty *gun* [sixty to ninety seconds], next add autumn sauce and boil for another twenty to thirty *gun* [sixty to ninety seconds], and finally add water to the chicken and again bring to a boil. Chop the napa cabbage into pieces. When the chicken is 70 percent done, add the chopped cabbage and boil it for the remaining 30 percent until the chicken is completely cooked. Season well with sugar and green onions. The cabbage must be boiled until completely done before the dish can be served. For each chicken, use four *liang* of oil.

---

19 The pear used here is the snow pear (*Pyrus nivalis*), with its crisp flesh that is similar to fresh bamboo shoots. It can be used as a sweet substitute for bamboo shoots in most stir-fry recipes, assuming you don't overcook it.

20 This recipe "imitates" the pheasant recipe later in this chapter, where the meat is seasoned, wrapped in caul fat, and fried. This in turn resembles the modern Taiwanese dish *ji juan* 雞卷 (chicken roll), a mixture of ground pork, onion, and egg wrapped inside tofu skin. Although the ingredients for the three dishes are somewhat different, the fillings cook to similar textures and consistencies, while the wrappings (tofu skin or caul fat) all fry up crisply.

Chicken Stir-Fried with Chestnuts[21]

Chop the chicken into pieces, and fry lightly in two *liang* of vegetable oil. To the chicken, add one rice bowl of *jiu*, one small cup of autumn sauce, one rice bowl of water, and braise until 70 percent done. Cook the chestnuts beforehand until tender and add them to the chicken along with the bamboo shoots, and continue braising until the chicken is fully done. Plate and garnish with a large pinch of sugar.

Seared Eight Pieces

Take a tender chicken and chop it into eight pieces. Fry them in oil until cooked. Pour away the oil, then add one cup of light soy sauce and half a *jin* of *jiu* to the chicken. Braise it until done and plate immediately. Do not use water. Cook using a strong flame.

Cluster of Pearls[22]

Chop cooked chicken breast into small morsels the size of soybeans and toss them evenly with light soy sauce and *jiu*. Roll the chicken in flour until each morsel is well coated, then stir-fry them in a wok using vegetable oil.

Huangqi 黃芪 (*Astragalus propinquus*, also known as Mongolian milkvetch) is an herb commonly used in Traditional Chinese Medicine. Only the root portion is used in this dish, for its purported expectorant and body strengthening properties.

Steamed Chicken with *Huangqi* Herbs for Curing Tuberculosis

Take a chicken that is still too young to lay eggs and slaughter it.[23] Do not rinse it with water. Remove the chicken's innards and stuff its cavity with one *liang* of *huangqi*. Place the chicken on a wok with a rack made of chopsticks to steam. Cover the wok and seal it well. When the chicken

---

21 This centuries-old recipe would fit right in on the dinner table of a modern Chinese family.

22 This is one of the more poetically-named dishes in the book. It refers to the look of the chicken pieces after they have been marinated, coated, and fried.

23 The terms used to describe chickens of different ages are a bit confusing. "Infant chickens" (*chuji* 雛雞) are younger than the "child chicken" (*tongji* 童雞) described here, which are in turn younger than "tender chicken" (*la ji* 嫩雞) used in the "Seared Eight Pieces" recipe above.

is done, remove it from the wok. The collected juices from the chicken are unctuous and savory, and can be used to treat weakness and fatigue resulting from the disease.

Braised Chicken

Take an entire chicken and stuff its body cavity with thirty stalks of green onion and two *qian* of fennel seeds. Use one *jin* of *jiu* and half a small cup of autumn sauce, and boil the chicken for one incense stick's time [one hour]. Next add one *jin* of water and two *liang* of rendered lard and braise everything together.[24] When the chicken is done, skim the fat off the cooking liquid. Be sure to use boiled water when braising. When the cooking liquid has been reduced down to a rice bowl full of thickened glaze, remove the chicken from the pot. The chicken can be served pulled apart by hand or sliced thinly with a knife, and then tossed and dressed with the glaze.

Jiang's Chicken

Take a young chicken and season it with four *qian* of salt, a spoon of soy sauce, half a teacup of aged *jiu*, and three large slices of ginger. Place it in a clay pot; steam it well, separated from the boiling water, until it is soft; then remove its bones. Do not add any water to the chicken when cooking. This is a recipe from the household of Census Officer Jiang.

Tang's Chicken

Take a chicken weighing either two or three *jin*. If it weighs two *jin*, use one rice bowl of *jiu* and three rice bowls of water. If it weighs three *jin*, increase the quantity of *jiu* and water accordingly. Cut the chicken into large pieces, then heat up two *liang* of vegetable oil. Thoroughly fry the chicken in the oil over high heat. Next, boil the fried chicken in the *jiu* for ten to twenty moments, then add the

---

24 An hour is a rather long time to braise chicken. And why add more water? Either chicken breeds were tougher in Yuan Mei's day or it may be another example of Yuan Mei's preference for cooking everything until it falls apart.

water and cook for another two to three hundred moments. Finally, add one wine cup of autumn sauce. When serving, add one *qian* of white sugar. This is a recipe from the household of Tang Jinghan.

Chicken Liver

Season the liver with *jiu* and vinegar while stir-frying. Chicken liver is best served tender.

Chicken Blood

Cut coagulated chicken blood into strips and cook them with chicken broth, soy sauce, vinegar, and starch noodles to make a thick soup. This dish is well suited to the elderly.[25]

Shredded Chicken

Pull the meat of chicken into shreds and toss it with autumn sauce, ground mustard, and vinegar. This is a Hangzhou dish. One can also add bamboo shoots and celery. Another method is to stir-fry the shredded chicken with shredded bamboo shoots, autumn sauce, and *jiu*. Use cooked chicken for the former "tossed" method, and raw chicken for the latter stir-fried method.

Chicken Cooked in Rice Lees

The way for making this chicken is the same as that for making pork cooked in lees.[26]

---

25 Blood is good for anemia as it is quite high in bioavailable iron. The fact that the red blood cells of chickens are nucleated also means that you get more nucleic acids than from the blood of other mammals. On top of that, it is far more smooth and supple than pork blood and better absorbs flavors from its cooking liquids. The way to coagulate chicken (or any animal) blood is as follows: Stir the blood while it is being collected and add a small amount of salt or brine. Pour the blood into a container and let it coagulate slightly. After that, place the blood in a steamer or double boiler and cook until done.

26 See the recipe "Pork Cooked in Lees" in the "Sacrificial Tribe" chapter.

Chicken Gizzards

Take thirty chicken gizzards and scald them in boiling water. Remove their tough membranes, then braise them in chicken broth with seasonings.[27] The delicate sweetness and tender textures of this dish are unrivaled.

Chicken Eggs

Break the eggs into a bowl and beat them with bamboo chopsticks a thousand times then steam until tender.[28] Eggs become tough when cooked, but with prolonged and continuous cooking they become tender again.[29] Those prepared with tea leaves should be cooked for a period of two sticks of incense [two hours]. To cook a hundred eggs, use two *liang* of salt; for fifty eggs use five *qian*.[30] One can also braise them with soy sauce. Other methods of preparation include pan-frying and stir- frying. Eggs steamed with shredded finch are also excellent.

Five Ways to Cook Pheasant[31]

Pull off the breast meat from a pheasant and season it well with light soy sauce. Wrap the breast meat in a sheet of caul fat and fry it in a flat-bottomed iron pot. The meat can be either wrapped as flat squares or as rolls. This is one method.

One can also slice the pheasant meat and stir-fry with seasonings or do so with diced breast meat. The whole pheasant can also be braised in the manner as for the domestic chicken. Another

---

27 Modern Chinese preparations do not typically braise the gizzards until tender. Rather the unique "crisp" texture of this muscle is enjoyed. One of the most renowned Chinese dishes that contain chicken gizzards is *youbao shuangcui* 油爆雙脆 (lit. oil-fried double crisp), which pairs its texture with the similar "crisp" texture of the of pork stomach.

28 The recipe for steamed egg (*zhudan* 蒸蛋) is quite similar to the Japanese chicken *chawanmushi*.

29 Yuan Mei's standards for "tough" and "tender" appear to be quite different from our modern criteria.

30 These two sentences briefly mention how to prepare tea eggs. The more complete recipe can be found later in the chapter "Scaleless Aquatic Creatures" ("Tea Egg") next to a good recipe for smoked eggs.

31 The Chinese word used here, *yeji*, actually encompasses almost any gallinaceous bird that is found wild. Translating it as pheasant is one possible option.

method is to first fry the meat in oil, then pull it apart into thin shreds, toss it with *jiu*, autumn sauce, vinegar, and mustard greens together as a cool salad.

Finally, one can also serve the raw meat sliced to be cooked in a hot pot and eaten immediately when done. The problem with this latter method is that when the meat is still tender, it lacks flavor, but by the time the flavor has infused the meat, it is already too tough.[32]

Red Simmered Chicken

To make red simmered chicken, first wash and clean out the bird well. For each *jin* of chicken, mix twelve *liang* of good *jiu*, two *qian* and five *fen* of salt, four *qian* of rock sugar, and finely ground cinnamon together in a clay pot. Braise it over a gentle charcoal fire. If the *jiu* has been simmered till dry but the chicken is still not soft, add a teacup of boiling water for each *jin* of chicken.

Braised Chicken with Mushrooms

Take a *jin* of chicken, a *jin* of sweet *jiu*, three *qian* of salt, four *qian* of rock sugar, and fresh mushrooms free of any mold. Braise everything over a gentle flame for a period of two incense sticks [two hours] until done. Do not add any water, and cook the chicken until 80 percent done before adding the mushrooms.

Pigeon[33]

Pigeon braised with good dry-cured ham is very good. One can also prepare it without the ham.

---

32 We can see from this that Yuan Mei is not completely averse to the hot pot after all (see section "Chafing Dishes" in the "Objectionables" chapter), though he is still critical of this type of cooking. Perhaps his aversion is culturally rooted, as chafing is one of the cooking techniques favored by the "barbaric" people from Mongolia and western Asia.

33 This could actually be any of the birds in genus *Columba*, including doves and pigeons. The word "squab" is used to refer to pigeons bred for food; typically, it implies a younger bird, but the Chinese ate predominantly adult ones.

Pigeon Eggs

Braised pigeon eggs are prepared in the same manner as braised chicken gizzards. They can also be pan-fried and served with a bit of vinegar.

Wild Duck

Cut the meat of the wild duck (mallard (*Anas platyrhynchos*) or Eurasian teal (*Anas crecca*)) into thick slices and season well with autumn sauce. Sandwich each slice of meat between two slices of snow pear and stir-fry them on both sides until done. The household of Circuit Intendant Mao of Suzhou was most apt at preparing this dish, but sadly that recipe has been lost. Wild duck can also be steamed in the same manner as steaming duck of the domesticated variety.

Steamed Duck

Remove the bones from a raw fat duck. Stuff the duck's body cavity with a mix consisting of one wine cup of glutinous rice, diced dried-cured ham, diced kohlrabi, shiitake, diced bamboo shoots, autumn sauce, *jiu*, warm-pressed sesame oil and chopped green onions. Place the duck on a plate and ladle chicken broth over

Warm-pressed oil is made using hot water to separate the oil instead of the typical roasting and hydraulic pressing. It has a gentler taste than regular sesame oil.

it. Steam the duck separated from water until thoroughly cooked. This recipe definitely comes from the household of Prefect Wei.

Duck in Disarray[34]

Take a fat duck and boil it in water until 80 percent done. When cool, remove its bones and tear the meat in both natural, disorderly

---

34 Considering that the duck is torn into random chunks and the yam is bashed into chunks, this dish could also be called "Canard à la Inhabile."

pieces, which are neither square nor round.[35] Place the meat back into its cooking liquid than add three *qian* of salt, half a *jin* of *jiu*, and also coarsely crushed mountain yam together into the pot to thicken the dish. When the meat is braised tender, add finely chopped ginger, shiitake, and chopped green onion. If one wants an especially thick soup, add powdered starch. The dish is also very good if one substitutes the mountain yam with taro instead.

Savory-Braised Duck

Do not use water, rather use *jiu* to braise the duck. Remove the bones and add seasonings before eating. This is a recipe from the household of Magistrate Yang of Gaoyao.

Duck Breast

Use the breast from a fat duck and chop it into large square pieces. Simmer it in half a *jin* of *jiu*, one cup of autumn sauce, bamboo shoots, shiitake, and chopped green onions. Reduce the cooking liquid and serve.

Cooking something at low heat with only a little liquid, is called *men* 燜 (lit. to suffocate, humid) in Chinese. Most of the actual cooking is done by the steam coming off the simmering liquid and the heat from the sides of the pot.

Roasted Duck

Take a young duck and mount it on a spit fork to roast.[36] The chef employed by Examiner Ping's household makes this exceptionally well.

Hanged Savory-Braised Duck

Stuff green onions into the duck's body cavity, cover the duck well, and braise it.

---

35 The term *bufang buyuan* 不方不圓 (not square, not round) is the opposite invocation of the Chinese ideal of "the heavens are round and the ground is square" (*tian yuan di fang* 天圓地方), meaning that the world is in order and harmonious.

36 A fork-roasted duck is probably similar to a so-called *pipa* duck, which is butterflied and flattened before it is put on the spit to roast. Of course, fork roasting could also be used when making something resembling the whole Cantonese roasted duck, although those are usually roasted on a hook.

Xu's store at Shuixi gate does this dish very well. This is a dish that cannot be made at home.[37] There are yellow and black variations of this braised duck; of the two, the yellow one is better.

Dry-Steamed Duck

This is the dry-steamed duck made at the household of Hangzhou merchant He Xingju. Wash a fat duck and chop it into eight chunks. Immerse the duck completely with sweet *jiu* and autumn sauce in a porcelain jar and seal it well.[38] Place everything directly in a dry pot to let "steam" over a low flame without adding water.[39] When it is ready to be served, the duck's meat should be as soft as mud. The dish takes the two incense sticks of time [two hours] to cook.

Wild Duck Meatballs

Chop the wild duck breast finely and add pork fat and a small amount of starch. Form the mixture into balls, and boil them in chicken broth. It is even better to use the original duck's broth instead. The household of Kong Qin from Daxing makes this exceptionally well.

Xu Duck[40]

Get the largest fresh duck available. Make a solution using twelve *liang* of *baihua* liquor, one *liang* and two *qian* of unrefined gray salt,[41] and a soup bowl of boiled water, removing any residue and froth

---

37 When something can't be made at home it is usually because the home kitchen does not have the specialized equipment, space, or facilities. In this case, maybe special equipment is needed to hang and braise the duck.

38 This is quite similar to how one would make a French cassoulet, *sans les haricots*.

39 This cooking technique is similar to the *men* 燜 method described in the recipe above (see also "Dry-Steamed Pork" in the "Sacrificial Animals" chapter).

40 The word *xu* 徐 literally means "slow," which describes the length of cooking here, but it could also be a family name, which would mean it is Xu's Duck. Due to the incomplete information, it is left untranslated.

41 Qingyan 青鹽 translates to "green" or "blue salt," which is a grayish-green raw salt more or less like the coarse grained *sel gris* of Guérande, France.

after dissolving everything, then apply this to the duck. Next replace the solution and add seven rice bowls of cold water and four thick slices of fresh ginger weighing approximately one *liang*, and place everything together inside a large lidded earthenware bowl. Seal the opening of the lidded bowl well using a sheet of thick paper and place everything on top of a large charcoal brazier to cook thoroughly.[42] Use large chunks of charcoal of three *yuan*,[43] each costing around two *wen*, for cooking, and cover the brazier and bowl with a tented cover so the heated air does not escape.[44] Cook, starting around the time one has breakfast until the evening. If the cooking is rushed, then the dish will be underdone and its flavors will be poorly developed. After the charcoal has burned through, do not change the duck to a serving bowl and do not open the sealed bowl too soon. After splitting the duck open, wash it with clean water, then dry it with a clean unstarched cloth before putting it into a lidded earthenware bowl.[45]

Braised Sparrow

Take fifty sparrows and braise them in light soy sauce and sweet *jiu*. When they are done, remove their feet, taking only the sparrows' meat from their breast and head, and put it into a dish with the cooking broth. The flavors are incredibly sweet and delicate. Other birds such as magpies can also be prepared thus. Unfortunately, fresh birds are hard to find.

---

42 This cooking method is similar to that seen in "Pork in a Lidded Bowl" in the "Sacrificial Animals" chapter.

43 In this context the *yuan* is either a chunk of the charcoal, or a volume unit similar to the English term "cord" used to measure firewood. As for the type of charcoal, what is clear is that *tanji* is of a premium grade considering that Yuan Mei specifies its high price. Perhaps this is a type of premium "white charcoal" 白炭 or a modern *jutan* 菊炭 used for fine barbecues and cooking in on-table braziers.

44 The phrase "cover the brazier and bowl with a tented cover so the heated air does not escape" implies that the cooking setup is covered using a stiff tent or umbrella-like structure. What this actually looks like remains unclear. If this was well-insulated, it would function like an oven.

45 This entire recipe is confusing, especially the last two sentences: don't change the bowl, but then take the duck out, wipe it dry, and put it back into another bowl. The fact that this recipe is still quite detailed likely means that Yuan Mei found it important enough to include, but on the whole, it is one of the more poorly written entries.

Xue Shengbai often advises, "Do not eat food made from domesticated animals," since the flavors of wild birds are more savory and fresh, and they are easier to digest.[46]

Braised Quail and Siskin

The quails (*Coturnix coturnix*) from Luhe District [in Nanjing] are the best. Prepared quails are also available. For siskin (*Spinus spinus*), braise using Suzhou wine lees, honey, and *jiu* until soft. Add to them the same seasonings used for braised sparrows.

Inspector Shen of Suzhou makes a braised siskin with bones that melt in the mouth, but its method of preparation is unknown. His stir-fried fish slices are also exceptional. With such incredible culinary skills, he can truly be ranked number one in all of Suzhou.

Yunlin Goose

In the poet Ni Zan's Yuan dynasty work, the *Yunlin Compendium*, he recorded a recipe for preparing geese. Take a whole goose, clean it, rub the inside of the body cavity with three *qian* of salt, and stuff with a large bundle of green onions such that the cavity is solidly filled. Cover the outside of the whole goose with a mixture of honey and *jiu*. In the pot, add a large bowl of *jiu* and a large bowl of water for steaming, and build a rack made of chopsticks to keep the goose elevated above the water. Use two bundles of mountain grass (e.g., sabai grass (*Eulaliopsis binata*), *Cymbopogon distans*, *Scleria levis*, or cogon grass (*Imperata cylindrica*)) as fuel for the stove, allow it to slowly and completely burn away. Wait for the pot to cool down completely, then open the lid, flip the goose over to its other side, replace the lid, and seal it well for steaming. Use one bundle of grass and allow it to fully burn.

The fuel should be allowed to burn on its own without any disturbance by the chef. The lid should be well sealed with cotton paper. If the sealing paper dries and cracks during cooking, simply moisten it with water.

---

46 There is some truth to this. Wild creatures have more varied diets and thus contain more diverse and rich micronutrients.

When it is ready to be served, the goose will be as soft as mud and its broth absolutely delectable. If duck is prepared using this technique, it will be just as delicious. Each bundle of the mountain grass used as fuel should weight one *jin* and eight *liang*. When one is rubbing the goose with salt, insert green onions, mix finely ground Sichuan pepper evenly with the *jiu*. The *Yunlin Compendium* contained numerous recipes, but after several trials this was the only good one; the rest of the recipes are simply false elaborations.

Roasted Goose

The roasted goose from Hangzhou is a culinary joke, given that it is more or less raw.[47] One's own chef could make it better at home.

---

47 Did people in Hangzhou make goose carpaccio or *tataki*?

WATER TRIBE

SCALED AQUATIC CREATURES

All fish require removal of their scales during preparation with only shad as the exception.[1] Being scaled creatures, I consider fish as a class on its own. Thus, the following are the recipes with scaled aquatic creatures.

---

[1] It is a tradition in Chinese cooking not to remove scales from shad. *Madam Wu's Recipe Book* (*Pujiang Wu shi zhong kui lu* 浦江吳氏中饋錄), a Song dynasty food manual, already indicated that when preparing a shad for steaming, one removes the innards but not the scales. It is unclear why this is done, though contemporary sources indicate that scaling shad removes some of its flavor, and that spitting out the scales while eating is actually part of the joy of eating this fish.

White Amur Bream

Take a live bream, add *jiu* and autumn sauce, then steam it. Cook until the flesh is translucent like jade. If it is cooked to an opaque white, the texture of the flesh becomes tough and its flavor changes for the worse. While steaming, cover everything well with a lid and do not let any condensing water drip onto the fish. When it is ready to be served, add shiitake and bamboo shoot tips.

Bream can also be prepared by pan-frying it with *jiu*. For this, use only *jiu* and not water. It is then knownn as "imitation shad."

Crucian Carp

One needs a certain level of expertise to buy crucian carp (*Carassius auratus*, common goldfish). Choose the ones that are flatter and with whiter skin because their tender and flaky flesh falls off the bones when cooked. Rounder and darker-skinned crucian carp have thick and hard bones. The innards of the fish must not be consumed.

It is best to prepare it steamed in the manner of the white amur bream. It is also good eaten pan-fried. The flesh can also be removed to make a thick soup. The people of Tongzhou District (Nantong) [in present-day Jiangsu Province] can braise crucian carp such that its bones and its tail become tender, a dish they call *suyu* [tender fish] that is well suited to be eaten by young children. Still, it cannot compare to the steamed version that presents the fish's true flavor.[2]

The carp from the Dragon Pond of Luhe District are large and tender, which is rather extraordinary. When steaming, use *jiu*, not water, and a small amount of sugar to enhance its delicate, savory flavor. Adjust the quantity of autumn sauce and *jiu* used according to the size of the fish.

---

2 Looking at the description of this tender fish (*suyu* 酥魚), it could be a variant of braised Crucian carp with scallions (*cong shao jiyu* 蔥燒鯽魚). That Yuan Mei claims this preparation cannot compare to the steamed version is quite like him. In the recipe for "Two Ways of Preparing Grenadier Anchovy" ("River Delicacies" chapter) he also complained that completely "tender fish" is terrible.

Topmouth Culter[3]

The flesh of the culter is the finest texture of all fish. It is best when steamed with shad that has been cured in rice lees. It is also very good lightly marinated during winter for two day in *jiu* and its lees. I once got a live culter just caught from the Yangzi and steamed it with *jiu*; it was delicious beyond words.[4] Culter goes best with wine lees but do not over-marinate it because doing so turns its meat dry.

Grouper

Groupers have few bones and are best when sliced and stir-fried. For stir-frying, the more thinly sliced the groupers' flesh, the better. Lightly season the fish with autumn sauce, then dredge it through starch powder and egg white before putting it into the wok, adding the appropriate seasonings while stir-frying. The oil of choice here is vegetable oil.

Dark Sleeper

In Hangzhou, dark sleepers are higher prized. Yet people in Jinling consider them worthless, and look upon them as tiger-headed snakes: with grotesque amusement. Its flesh is very tender and soft, and it can be pan-fried, boiled, or steamed. It can also be cooked with pickled mustard greens as a remarkable delicate and delicious thick soup.

Odontobutis obscura, a fish from the goby sub-order. Dark sleeper sounds like some dormant monster, though in reality it is a shy fish that hides at the bottom of shallow waters.

---

3 *Baiyu* 白魚 literally means "white fish," which is a rather ambiguous name, given that there are numerous fish with that name in Chinese. Looking at several Chinese classics on herbal medicine, "white fish" likely comes from *boyu* 鉑魚 (mentioned in the *Zhen Nan bencao* 滇南本草) which eventually became known as *jiaoyu* 鱎魚 in the *Compendium of Materia Medica* (published 140 years after the *Zhen Nan bencao*). All these names are scientific references to indicate the topmouth or red-fin culter. It does not help that this culter is in turn known by numerous Latin names, among them *Erythroculter ilishaeformis* and *Culter alburnus*. According to the *Encyclopedia of Life*, however, its accepted scientific name is *Chanodichthys erythropterus*.

4 Yuan Mei's actual words on the flavors of the fish are "so beautiful I could not describe it" (*mei bu ke yan* 美不可言), which says a lot considering his skill with words.

Fish Floss[5]

Grass carp is native to China and was only recently introduced in the United States, where it was used as a control measure against aquatic plants. This species of fish has molar-like teeth to feed on and chew up tough algae and plants. Being a robust and adaptable species, however, they are now overpopulating the Mississippi River.

Steam black carp (*Mylopharyngodon piceus*) or grass carp (*Ctenopharyngodon idella*) until done and pull the meat off the bones. Fry the meat in a wok until golden brown, then add fine salt, green onion, Sichuan pepper, soy-pickled cucumbers, and soy-pickled ginger. When stored in a sealed jar during winter, this can last a whole month.

Fish Balls[6]

Use either a live topmouth culter or black carp, split the fish in half, and nail it to a board. Use a knife and scrap off the meat, leaving the bones and spine on the board. Chop the meat until fine, mix with lard and bean starch, then stir the mixture with one's hand. Add a little salt water, but do not use light soy sauce. Add green onions and ginger juice, and form the mixture into balls. When this is done, place them in boiling water to cook. Scoop them out when done, and let them rest in a bath of cold water. When they are ready to be served, boil them with chicken broth and laver.

Fish Slices

Take slices of black carp or grouper, season with autumn sauce, and then add starch powder and egg white. Start a wok and stir-fry the slices over high heat. Plate them on a small dish, and add green onions, Sichuan pepper, soy-pickled cucumbers, and soy-pickled ginger. Each dish should not contain more than six *liang* of fish,

---

5 This fish floss is similar to the commonly found dried-meat (pork) floss.

6 This is a very accurate and detailed description for making fish balls and one of the more complete recipes by Yuan Mei.

since heat cannot be evenly and thoroughly applied when there are too many ingredients.

Silver Carp with Tofu

Pan-fry a large silver carp until done, add tofu, spray on soy sauce, water, green onions, and *jiu*, and then boil everything. When the color of the soup has turned slightly red in hue, it is ready to be served.

The flavor from the fish's head is incredibly good. This is a Hangzhou dish. The amount of soy sauce to be used here is proportional to the size of the fish.

Fish Embraced by Vinegar

Chop a live black carp into large pieces, sear them in oil, add soy sauce and vinegar, and spray with *jiu*, with the more broth the better. When done, immediately remove from the pan. This dishwas most famously prepared by the House of Five Willows, at Hangzhou's West Lake. But ever since they started using an ill-smelling soy sauce, the fish served there is now inedible. What a pity!

The fame of Madame Song's fish soup[7] is not warranted at all. The discussions in *Records on Dreams of Millet* should also not be believed.

The chosen fish must not be big; the flavors will not penetrate into a big fish. The chosen fish must also not be small, since small fish tend to have more spiny bones.

Icefish[8]

When icefish are just caught fresh from the water, they are known as a "savory of ice." Braise them in chicken broth with dried-cured

---

7 The famed fish soup from Madame Song consisted of small pieces of fish cooked in a thick and rich soup punctuated by vinegar.

8 Although the literal translation of the Chinese word used is "silver fish," Yuan Mei's indication that this fish looks like ice points to *Salanx prognathus*. This species of icefish, found in the freshwaters of China, retains in adulthood many of the features present in a fish's larval stages. They are

Diluted soy sauce (*jiangshui* 醬水, lit. sauce water) can be soy sauce diluted with water or the liquid extracted from a wet bean sauce.

ham. Alternatively, stir-fry them for a more tender fish. For the dried item, soak them in water until soft. They make a good dish when stir-fried with diluted soy sauce.

Taixiang (Dried Salted Fish)

There are many differences between good and bad *taixiang*. That which comes from Songmen of Taizhou is the best, with its soft but savory and rich-tasting flesh. When the raw item is pulled to shreds by hand, it can be served directly as a side dish without cooking.

When braising with fresh pork, first wait until the pork has softened before adding the *taixiang*, otherwise the *taixiang* would have long melted away and no longer be visible. When this dish is chilled, it becomes *xiang* aspic. This is a Shaoxing recipe.

Dried Salted Fish in Wine Lees

In the winter, salt a large common carp and dry it. Cover it with wine lees and place it in an earthenware jar, then seal the jar's opening.[9] Serve it in the summer. Do not use distilled liquors to prepare this dish, since it would have the harsh stinging of the liquor.

This dish is known in Japan as *nishikyosukedo* 西京漬など, and is similar to Japanese *kasuzuke*.

Shrimp on Dried Salted Shad

During the summer, choose a white, clean, belt-like dried shad (*Ilisha elongata*, slender shad) and soak it in water for a day to remove its salty taste. Dry it under the sun and pan-fry with oil. When one

---

small, translucent, largely cartilaginous fish, and as such, they look like whitebait and sometimes are mistaken as such. They are sometimes known as "noodle fish," because their form and texture resemble thick rice noodles.

9 Fish prepared this way is known in Japan as *nishikyosukedo* 西京漬など, and this dish is similar to Japanese *kasuzuke*.

side of the fish is golden brown, remove it from the pan. Place shrimp on the side of the fish that has not been fried, then put everything on a plate, add white sugar, and steam for the time of one stick of incense [one hour] until done. This dish is perfect for late summer.

Fish Jerky

Remove the head and tail of a live black carp. Chop the fish into small square pieces, thoroughly marinate it with salt and dry it in the wind. Pan-fry it in a wok, add seasonings, and reduce any juices from cooking. Next, stir-fry some sesame, toss with the fish, and serve. This is a Suzhou recipe.[10]

Home-Style Pan-Fried Fish

To make home-style pan-fried fish, one needs patience. Wash a grass carp until clean, chop it into pieces, and marinate it with salt. Flatten each piece and fry both sides until golden brown, then add a good quantity of *jiu* and autumn sauce and simmer slowly over a low flame. When it is nearly done, finish by reducing the cooking liquid, ensuring that all the flavors from the seasonings have entered the fish.

This recipe is only for preparing fish that are already dead. For live fish, it is best to cook it rapidly.[11]

---

10 Two very different dishes can come from this recipe, all depending on how well dried the fish is. If it is only lightly dried, then it would be similar to some of the dried chicken and pork dishes mentioned in previous sections. If the fish was thoroughly dried, however, then this would be more like a snack.

11 While this is not a particularly unusual way of preparing fish, Yuan Mei's comments on preparing dead and live fish allow us a bit of insight. First, that this recipe is for cooking dead fish, while previous fish recipes use only live fish, points to the differences in techniques for cooking each one well. Second, this recipe is titled "home style," implying that in most households it was uncommon to prepare live fish, whether because of convenience or financial reasons. Indeed, the best-tasting fish is bought alive and then slaughtered just before cooking, but keeping fish alive for cooking is rather tedious, and more expensive.

Huanggu Fish

In modern usage, *huanggu* fish refers to the yellow drum (*Nibea albiflora*), a relative of the yellow croaker. Smaller specimens of this fish are sold dried all around Zhejiang and Anhui provinces.

Huizhou [She Prefecture, Anhui Province] produces a small fish around two to three inches in length that is sold and delivered in dried form. Prepare by adding *jiu* to them, removing their skins, and placing them on top of a rice pot to steam. This dish, known as *Huanggu* fish, is most savory and delicious.

WATER TRIBE

SCALELESS AQUATIC CREATURES

Fish lacking scales smell significantly fishier. Thus, they require much greater attention in their preparation. Their shortcomings can be overcome through the judicious use of ginger and cinnamon. The following is a collection of recipes with scaleless aquatic creatures.

Eel in Broth

It is best to avoid cooking eel with its bones removed. The item is naturally fishy in smell, but one should not over manipulate or attempt to control it, lest we risk losing its natural character. Like Reeves shad, it should not be cooked without its scales.

To prepare it plain braised, take a river eel, wash away its slime, and chop it into inch-long segments. Put them in an earthenware jar and braise with *jiu* and water until soft. Add autumn sauce when it is ready to serve. One can also make a soup with it using newly preserved mustards prepared during winter, along with large amounts of green onion and ginger to rid the eel of its fishiness.

I also remember well that a certain imperial government official's household braised it with thickening starch and mountain yam for a good dish. It can also be seasoned and directly placed on a plate for steaming without adding any water in the dish. Official Jia Zhihua makes the best steamed eel. Add four *dui* [units] of soy sauce and six *dui* [units] of *jiu*, making sure to use just enough broth to cover the body of the eel. The steaming time must be well judged and controlled, since over-steaming would cause the eel's skin to wrinkle and its flesh to lose flavor.

The exact amount of a *dui* is uncertain, but it is used here to specify a certain ratio of *jiu* to soy sauce. The exact amount appears irrelevant, as long as the fish is covered with the wine and soy sauce mixture.

Red-Cooked Eel

Braise the eel in *jiu* and water until soft, adding sweet sauce instead of the usual autumn sauce. Reduce the broth, add fennel seeds and star anise, then plate. There are three common errors when preparing this eel dish. First, the skin becomes marked by wrinkles and folds, thus rendering the skin not tender. Second, its flesh falls apart in one's bowl, making it impossible to pick up with chopsticks. Finally, if salted fermented beans are added too early when cooking, the eel's flesh will no longer be tender. The household of Officer Zhu from Yangzhou is most skilled in making this dish. In general, red-cooked eel is best when its cooking juices are reduced, which allows the flavors to be fully absorbed into the flesh of the eel.

Fried Eel

Choose a large eel, remove its head and tail, and chop it into inch-long segments. First, fry them in sesame oil until thoroughly cooked and place them on the side. Take the tender tips of fresh chrysanthemum greens (*Glebionis coronaria*) and stir-fry them until done, using the oil previously used to cook the eel. Next, place the eel on top of the greens, season, and braise them for one incense stick of time [one hour].[1] The quantity of chrysanthemum greens used should be about half that of the eel.

Raw Stir-Fried Soft-Shell Turtle

Remove the bones from a soft-shell turtle (*Pelodiscus sinensis*), and stir-fry it over high heat using sesame oil. Add one cup of autumn sauce and one cup of chicken broth. This recipe most definitely comes from the household of Prefect Wei.

Soft-Shell Turtle Stir-Fried with Soy Sauce

Parboil a soft-shell turtle, remove its bones, heat up a wok, and stir-fry it over high heat. Add soy sauce, water, green onions, and Sichuan pepper, reduce the cooking liquid to a sauce then plate. This is a Hangzhou recipe.

Bone-in Soft-Shell Turtle

Take a soft-shell turtle weighing half a *jin* and chop it into four pieces. Add three *liang* of rendered lard to a heated wok and panfry

---

1 This means the chrysanthemum greens are cooked until brown and mushy.

the turtle so that the pieces are golden brown on both sides. Braise with water, autumn sauce, and *jiu*, first with a hot flame then a gentle flame. Add garlic when the turtle is 80 percent done. Before plating, add green onion, ginger, and sugar. When choosing a soft-shell turtle for this dish, prefer smaller ones to larger ones. It is only those small turtles colloquially known as "boy's foot turtle" that are sufficiently tender.

Soft-Shell Turtle with Gray Salt

Chop a soft-shell turtle into four pieces and stir-fry it thoroughly in a hot wok. For every *jin* of the turtle, braise it with four *liang* of *jiu*, three *qian* of star anise, and one and a half *qian* of salt until half done. Add two *liang* of rendered lard, and chop the turtle into the pieces the size of azuki beans before continuing to braise, adding garlic and bamboo shoot tips. Before plating, add green onion and Sichuan pepper. One can add autumn sauce before plating, but never add salt. This is a recipe from the household of Tang Jinghan of Suzhou. Large soft-shell turtles are tough, and small ones smell fishy. It is best to buy one that is medium in size.

Soup-Braised Soft-Shell Turtle

Boil a soft-shell turtle in water, remove its bones, and tear the meat into pieces. Braise it in chicken broth, autumn sauce, and *jiu*, reducing the liquid from two bowls until there is one bowl, plate the soup and blend it with green onions, Sichuan pepper, and ground ginger. The household of Wu Zhuyu prepares this dish extremely well. Use a small amount of starch such that the prepared soup is sufficiently thick.

Whole-Shell Soft-Shell Turtle

In the household of General Yang from Shandong, they prepare soft-shell turtle by removing its head and tail, portioning off its meat and the turtle's soft "skirt" to braise with seasonings, and then covering everything with the turtle shell.

At the banquet, each guest would be served a small plate with a single turtle cooked in this manner. Those presented with the turtle would be completely startled by its appearance, concerned they had been served something still alive and moving. Sadly the method for the dish's preparation is lost.

Shredded Rice Eel Soup

Boil the rice eel until it is half done, then slice it into thin shreds, and remove its bones. Braise in *jiu* and autumn sauce. Add a small amount of starch powder along with daylily flower, winter melon, and long green onions to finish into a thick soup. The chefs in Nanjing like to grill rice eels until they are charred, which is impossible to understand.

Stir-Fried Rice Eel

Tear the rice eel into thin shreds and stir-fry until slightly browned, in the same manner as stir-frying chicken. Do not add water.

Rice Eel Segments

Cut the rice eel into inch-long pieces and braise them in the same manner as eel. It can also be fried first in oil to firm up its flesh, and then accompanied by winter melon, fresh bamboo shoots, and shiitake. Use only a small amount of diluted soy sauce and larger amounts of ginger juice.

Shrimp Balls

Shrimp balls are made in the same way as fish balls. They can be either braised in chicken broth or stir-fried dry. When pounding the shrimp to a paste, be sure not to make it too fine, otherwise its original flavors and textures would be lost. This is the same with fish balls.[2] The shrimp can also be peeled whole and mixed with laver, making a great dish.

---

2 This is somewhat surprising since modern fish balls tend to be rather homogenous and fine in texture.

Shrimp Cakes

Pound the shrimp into a paste, form into balls and panfry. These are known as shrimp cakes.

Drunken Shrimp

Panfry the whole shrimp with shells and *jiu* over high heat until yellow, then remove from the pan.[3] Apply an appropriate amount light soy sauce and rice vinegar. When done, cover the shrimp with the bowl to cook with its residual heat. When ready to serve, place them in a dish. Their shells should be tender enough to be eaten.

Stir-Fried Shrimp

Stir-fried shrimp is done in the same manner as stir-fried fish and can be cooked with garlic chives. It can also be cooked with mustard greens pickled during the winter if one cannot eat garlic chives. There is also a recipe where the body of the shrimp is pounded flat and stir-fried on its own that was quite novel and interesting.

Crab

Crabs are best eaten on their own without accompaniment. They are best boiled in lightly salted brine and most enjoyable when shelled by the eaters themselves. Although crab cooked by steaming is fuller in flavor, it is much too plain to be enjoyable.

Crab Soup

Shell a crab and make a thick soup from the meat, using its juices for braising. Do not add any chicken extracts because crab is

---

3 Since the range of colors covered by the Chinese term *huang* 黃 goes from the palest hue of yellow to a dark earthy brown, the "yellow" *jiu* (*huang jiu* 黃酒) used in cooking the shrimp would likely be dark yellow, even brownish in color. This is a very different drunken shrimp compared to the modern version of this recipe, which is basically shrimp marinated in *jiu*.

best when cooked on its own. I've seen vulgar chefs adding duck tongue, shark's fin, or sea cucumber, which not only robs the crab of its flavors but adds an irritating fishiness to the dish. A complete abomination!

Stir-Fried Crabmeat[4]

It is best to stir-fry crabmeat that has just been shelled. Four hours after shelling, the crabmeat would have dried up and lost its flavor.

Steamed Shelled Crab

Shell an entire crab, take its meat, tomalley, and roe, and stuff it inside the carapace. Place five or six stuffed crabs on top of raw eggs and steam. When served at the table, the crab looks whole, minus its claws and legs. This feels like a more novel take on stir-fried crabmeat. Magistrate Yang Lanpo mixes pumpkin with crab, which is rather unusual.

Venus Clams

Venus clams (family *Veneridae*, Manila clams or Asian hard clams) are very good shucked and stir-fried with garlic chives. They can also be cooked as a soup. Overcooking will make them dry and tough.

Cockles

Cockles can be prepared in three ways. Splash with boiling water, and when they are half done, remove one shell and marinate them

---

4 Here, crabmeat (*xiefan* 蟹粉, lit. crab powder) refers to the meat, roe, tomalley, and other soft edible bits that have been shelled and picked out from the crab rather than just the loose whitish crabmeat that one can buy in supermarkets in the West. Crabmeat from the Chinese mitten crab is a thick, fragrant, bright orange-yellow mass, due to the large amounts of crab tomalley and roe mixed in with the meat. This dish is likely what Yuan Mei's imitation crab recipe was trying to imitate (see "Imitation Crab" in the "River Delicacies" chapter).

in *jiu* and autumn sauce until they are "drunk."[5] Or they can be cooked in chicken broth by removing one shell and putting them into the broth. Finally, they can also be fully shucked and made into a thick soup. It is best to cook them quickly as overcooking will leave them dry and tough. Cockles are produced in Fenghua Prefecture and should be preferred over giant clams and Venus clams.

Giant Clam[6]

Slice some pork belly, then simmer them with the right seasonings until soft. Wash the clam (genus *Tridacna* or *Hippopus*) and stir-fry with sesame oil, then add the pork slices and their juices to cook. One should add more autumn sauce when cooking so there is sufficient flavor. Tofu can also be added, if desired.

Giant clams are produced in Yangzhou. Due to concerns over spoilage, they usually are sold shucked and preserved in lard so that they can endure longer transport.[7] The sun-dried item is also very good. When cooked in chicken broth, they are much better than dried razor clams. Giant clams can also be pounded until tender and flat as a pancake, then pan-fried and eaten like a shrimp cake. These are good with seasonings added.

Cheng Zegong's Dried Razor Clams

The merchant house of Cheng Zegong produces dried razor clams (family *Solenidae*), prepared by soaking them in cold water for a day,

---

5 There is no mention of any applied heat to cook the cockles, but what's likely happening here is that they are being cooked over a low flame with a few splashes of hot water. Marinating shellfish in this manner is still commonly practiced in many Chinese cuisines. In Taiwan, smooth pumpkin-seed-sized clams are marinated in *jiu* and soy sauce with large amounts of garlic and chilies to make a popular appetizer.

6 The thick shells of these clams are also carved and polished into beads for jewelery and treated as a type of gemstone.

7 This is an interesting method of preservation, similar to the ways of making French rillettes or English potted meats.

boiling for two days, and squeezing out their liquid five times.[8] A one-inch-long dried item, once rehydrated will be two inches long with the appearance of a fresh razor clam, which can then be braised in chicken broth. People from Yangzhou try to learn the method of its preparation, but they cannot make it better than Cheng's household.

Fresh Razor Clams

The cooking method of razor clams is similar to that of giant clams. They can be stir-fried. The household of He Chunchao makes such an incredible tofu in razor clam broth that it can be considered a masterpiece.

Due to the similarity in their texture and taste, frogs are called "water chicken" (*shuiji* 水雞) in Chinese. They are also known as "paddy chicken" (*tianji* 田雞) since they are commonly found in the flooded fields where rice is grown.

Frogs

Remove the body of the frog and use only the legs. First sear them in hot oil, add autumn sauce, sweet wine, soy-pickled cucumbers, and soy-pickled ginger, then serve. Its meat can also be pulled off and stir-fried. It tastes like chicken.

Side dishes are usually salty, and strong-flavored, for example stewed gluten, chili, bamboo shoot, or soy-pickled cucumbers. A traditional Chinese or Japanese breakfast usually consists of several side dishes with a bowl of rice or congee.

Smoked Eggs[9]

Braise chicken eggs with seasonings until done. Slowly smoke them dry, then slice and serve them on a plate as a side dish.

8 This must be a texture food, similar to deer tendon, due to the complicated preparation method with all the soaking, boiling, and squeezing.

9 These two egg recipes are likely placed in this section by mistake. The printer probably misplaced them, and they should have been at the end of the "Winged Tribe" chapter. A less likely explanation would be that in the minds of Qing dynasty literati, eggs are somehow conceptually grouped with these critters.

Tea eggs are one of the most commonly eaten Chinese snacks and can be found in every neighborhood in China. In Taiwan, they are sold in convenience stores next to the *oden*, a Japanese winter food consisting of various items simmered in soup stock.

Tea Eggs

Take one hundred chicken eggs, add one *liang* of salt and coarse tea leaves. Boil for two incense sticks' of time [two hours] until done. If there are only fifty eggs, add five *qian* of salt, increasing or decreasing the quantities of ingredients as required. They can be eaten as a snack.

A Note on Vegetables

Saying that rich and well-connected people prefer vegetarian fare conversely implies that only the poor, powerless, or the newly rich crave meat—which is not to say that the vegetable dishes preferred by the wealthy of Yuan Mei's time aren't heavily flavored with meats and seafood. Quite the opposite; many use concentrated broths and extracts from countless animals just to infuse tofu and vegetables with rich savory flavors. Against the backdrop of rampant starvation in China at the time, it is hard to imagine the elite using the meat and bones of chickens and pigs just to make a broth to flavor some vegetable dish, then tossing all the other meat ingredients, or giving them to the servants and the poor. Also, the tofu recipes in this section contain some of the most elegantly wasteful and refined court dishes that Yuan Mei likely had during his lifetime.

Earth Tribe

Assorted Vegetable Dishes: Greens, Beans, and Tofu

Dishes can be split into those that are meat-based or vegetable-based, just like clothes can be split into those worn over or under other garments. The privileged and wealthy indulge themselves more on vegetable dishes than they do on meat-based dishes. The following are the assorted vegetable recipes.

Assistant Minister Jiang's Tofu

Remove the skin on both sides of each piece of tofu, cut each into sixteen slices, sun-dry them slightly, and simmer in rendered lard, only adding the tofu when whiffs of smoke appear over the lard. Sprinkle a large pinch of salt on the tofu, flip them, then add a teacup of good sweet *jiu* and 120 large dried shrimp. If one does not have large dried shrimp, use three hundred small dried shrimp instead.[1] The dried shrimp must be first boiled and then soaked for two hours. Next add a small cup of autumn sauce, let the tofu boil for a moment, then add a large pinch of sugar, and let boil for another while. Finally, add 120 segments of thin green onions, each half an inch long, and plate at a leisurely pace.[2]

Yang Zhongcheng's Tofu

Take tender tofu and cook it [in water] to rid it of its bean-like smell,[3] next put it into chicken broth, and briefly boil with abalone slices. Add lees sauce and shiitake, then plate the dish. The chicken extract used must be quite concentrated, and the abalone must be thinly sliced.[4]

Dry stir-frying (*ganchao* 乾炒) is a technique that involves stir-frying with oil but without the addition of water (or any other liquid) during the cooking process.

Zhang Kai's Tofu

Pound the dried shrimp until they are pulverized, then add them to tofu. Heat up an oiled wok and dry stir-fry everything with seasoning.

---

1 With this amount of dried shrimp, these are either rather large pieces of tofu, or this dish uses as much dried shrimp as tofu.

2 This recipe is quite detailed, even prescribing the number of pieces of green onion to add to the dish. Maybe it is important to have the exact same number of green onion segments as pieces of shrimp?

3 The text does not directly mention the use of water, but in the context of "cooking" (*zhu* 煮), water was most likely involved. The procedure for preparing the Hibiscus Tofu recipe below supports this reading.

4 For short cooking times, abalone must be sliced as thin as flakes, or else it will be too tough. Either that or the abalone has to be precooked.

Qing Yuan's Tofu

Take a teacup of *douchi*, soak them in water until very soft, then add them to tofu and stir-fry them together in a wok.

Hibiscus Tofu

Take *douhua* (tofu jelly),[5] add boiling water to it and soak three times to rid it of its bean-like smell. Add it to chicken broth at medium boil. When plating, add laver and peeled shrimp.

Prefect Wang's Eight Treasure Tofu

Take tender tofu, then slice and cut it until it has been minced thoroughly into fine particles. Add to it finely minced[6] shiitake, mushrooms, pine nuts, melon seeds, chicken, and dry-cured ham. Put everything into concentrated chicken extract, and stir the mixture until it boils, then plate and serve.[7] One can also use *douhua* [tofu jelly]. Eat this with a spoon and not with chopsticks.

Prefect Meng Ting recounted, "The recipe for this dish was bestowed by the Sagely Forefather [Emperor Kangxi of the Qing dynasty] to Minister Jian An. When the Minister went to acquire the recipe, the imperial kitchens charged him one thousand taels of silver." The Prefect's ancestor was Master Lou Cun, who was born to the aforementioned minister, which is how he got the recipe.[8]

Cheng Liwan's Tofu

During the twenty-third year of Emperor Qianlong [1759], I visited the home of Cheng Liwan in Yangzhou with [the writer and

---

5 Douhua 豆花 (bean flower), sometimes translated as "tofu jelly" or "tofu flower," is the more popular name of a soy product one gets immediately after curdling soy milk. In Chinese, it is also called rotten brain (*funao* 腐腦), as it is soft and tender like brains.

6 Xue 屑 literally means "crumbs" or "bits" but is translated as "finely minced." It is not the most accurate translation but indicates the even fineness that one gets by cutting in an orderly manner.

7 This feels like a more tedious version of shredded tofu (*wensi doufu* 文思豆腐). While for shredded dishes all ingredients need to be cut into fine threads, this recipe requires another set of cuts to "dice" all the ingredients into bits less than one millimeter.

8 This is an actual recipe from the imperial kitchens.

painter] Jin Shoumen and had a pan-fried tofu that was unparalleled in deliciousness. The tofu was dry and golden brown on both sides without even a touch of cooking liquid. It also had a hint of the delicate savoriness one finds in the giant clam, yet there was no giant clam or any other ingredients to be found in the dish.[9]

The next day I told Cha Xuanmen about this, and he proudly stated, "Oh, I can make the dish! I'm going to invite you over especially to try it." Thus, I went together with [the scholar] Hang Shijun to eat at Cha's place.

As we reached with our chopsticks to try it, we broke out in laughter. Before us was a dish made with chicken and sparrow brains without any tofu to be seen. It was so greasy and nauseating that it proved hard to stomach. The cost of this dish was also ten times that of Cheng's, but the flavors were not even close.

Sadly at the time, I had to quickly depart due to the death of my younger sister and lacked the time to ask Cheng for the recipe. Cheng passed away after a year, leaving me with much regret. Now all I have is the name of this dish. Still, I will ask for the recipe when opportunity comes.[10]

Frozen Tofu

Freeze tofu for one night, cut into square pieces, and boil them to rid them of their bean-like smell. Add them to a mixture of chicken broth and extracts, ham extract, and pork extract, and braise. When serving, remove the chicken and ham and the like, leaving only the shiitake and the winter bamboo shoots.[11] When tofu has been braised for a long time, its texture becomes spongy, with its surface honeycombed like that of frozen tofu. For stir-frying, use soft

---

9 The tofu was probably boiled and marinated in concentrated clam broth or extract before being lightly air-dried and pan-fried.

10 This reads like a diary entry (there isn't even a recipe) of Yuan Mei visiting his friends to shoot the breeze, leading to a cooking contest. The people Yuan Mei ate with were likely all political and literary figures of the time.

11 The shitake and bamboo shoots were not mentioned earlier. Either Yuan Mei forgot them or he considered them self-evident.

tofu, while braising should be done with firmer tofu.[12] The household of Officer Jia Zhihua cooks tofu with mushrooms; even during the summer they follow the same recipe for frozen tofu, since it is very good. Do not use strong-flavored *hun* [pork or beef] broths for this dish, since doing so would destroy the delicate light flavors of this dish.

Hun 葷 is an umbrella term used in Chinese culture to describe ingredients with a strong and rank smell (or flavor), including meat, onions, and garlic. Traditionally, it indicates the items that some Buddhist are not allowed to eat.

Shrimp-Sauce Tofu

Use an aged shrimp sauce to substitute for the light soy sauce when stir-frying tofu. Both sides of the tofu should be seared until golden brown. The wok must be hot. Cook with rendered lard, green onions, and Sichuan pepper.

Chrysanthemum Greens

Sear the chrysanthemum greens' tips in hot oil until they start shriveling, then add them to chicken broth to boil. When ready to plate, add a hundred stalks of pine mushroom (*Lactarius deliciosus*).

Fiddleheads

When preparing fiddleheads (bracken fern (*Pteridium aquilinum*) or nest fern (*Asplenium nidus*)), one must not be frugal; first remove all the fern's mature branches and leaves, keeping only the straight shoots. Rinse them until clean and simmer until soft,[13] then braise them in chicken broth. Buy only those from northern China, since those are the plumpest.

---

12 This does not apply exclusively to frozen tofu.

13 This describes the important process of parboiling to leach some of the noxious, possibly carcinogenic substances out of the fern.

Pearl Algae

The Chinese name for morels is *yangdu cai* 羊肚菜 and means "sheep stomach vegetable," referring to the tripe-like appearance of the mushroom's cap. Stone hair is a species of strip-like or filamentous algae (*Ulva compressa*) found growing on coastal rocks and boulders. Finally, Loosestrife (*Lysimachia clethroides*) is called "pearl greens" (*zhenzhu cai* 珍珠菜) in Chinese.

Carefully pick through the pearl algae (*Nostoc commune* var. *sphaeroides* or *Nostoc pruniforme*) to clean it. Boil until somewhat soft, then braise in chicken and ham broth. When serving the dish, it is best when only the pearls are visible and not the chicken or the ham used in its preparation. The household of provincial official Tao excels at preparing this dish.

Morels

Morels are produced in Hubei Province. They are prepared in the same manner as pearl algae.

Stone Hair

The preparation is the same as pearl algae. During summer, it is especially good mixed with sesame oil, vinegar, and autumn sauce.

Loosestrife Greens

The preparation is the same as chrysanthemum greens. They are produced in Xin'an County [Luoyang, Henan Province] upstream of the Yangtze (Chang) River.

Roasted Vegetarian Goose[14]

Boil mountain yam until soft, cut it into inch-long pieces, and wrap in tofu skin. Pan-fry in oil, then add autumn sauce, *jiu*, sugar,

---

14 This recipe is a remarkably poor substitute for goose and requires quite an imaginative effort on the diner's part.

soy-pickled cucumbers, and soy-pickled ginger, and cook until brownish red in color.

Garlic Chives[15]

Garlic chives are strong-flavored. Reserve the white portions of garlic chives and stir-fry with dried shrimp for a great dish. They are also good stir-fried with fresh shrimp, soft-shell turtle, or pork.

Celery

Celery is a *su* [vegetarian] food item. The plumper it is, the better it tastes. Choose the white stalks to stir-fry, add bamboo shoots, and cook until done. People now like to stir-fry it with pork, confusing its flavor and rendering it largely undefinable.[16] When not fully cooked, celery is quite crisp but flavorless. When mixed raw with pheasant, it is quite the dish to laud over.[17]

Su 素 (vegetarian) is the opposite of *hun* 葷, indicating ingredients (or dishes) without animal products or strong-smelling vegetables like garlic, onions, shallots, or garlic chives.

Bean Sprouts

I am rather fond of the soft, crisp textures of bean sprouts. When stir-fried, they must be cooked until completely done in order for the flavors from the seasonings to combine harmoniously with them.

Bean sprouts can be used with bird's nest, with their soft textures and white colors matching each other well. Still, there are many people who ridicule this recipe, since it pairs an incredibly cheap ingredient with an exceedingly expensive one. Clearly they do not understand that those such as Chao and Yu went on

---

15 Disappointingly little is said here about this very tasty and easy-to-grow vegetable.

16 The flavor of celery is often strong enough to cut through any meat, while simultaneously enhancing its flavor much like ginger does.

17 This preparation is similar to the classic home-style chicken with celery.

to respectively accompany the mythological Emperors Yao and Shun.[18]

Jiao (Wild-Rice Stems)[19]

Jiaobai can be stir-fried with pork or chicken. These shoots are very good when cut into pieces and grilled or seared with soy sauce and vinegar. They are also very good when simmered with pork.[20] Before cooking, the shoots must be sliced into inch-long pieces for the best effect. Shoots that are too thin have no flavor.

Qingcai (Green Vegetables)[21]

Tender qingcai can be stir-fried with bamboo shoots. During the summer, dress it with ground mustard and a little vinegar to awaken one's appetite. One can make a soup with it using dried-cured ham. One must look for those that have been freshly picked to ensure that they will be soft and tender.

Taicai (Mustard Greens)

Stir-fried taicai stems are quite tender.[22] Remove its outer skin, then add mushrooms and new bamboo shoots to make a soup. It is very good stir-fried with shelled shrimp.

---

18 This sentence refers to a line in the Book of Han (Scroll 72): "Above are Yao and Shun, below are Chao and Yu." During their rule, the two mythological emperors Yao and Shun were aided by Chao (Chaofu 巢父) and Yu (Yuyou 許由). Chao was a Daoist, and Yu a hermit, and both were eventually offered the throne by Yao, but they both refused.

19 Jiaobai 茭白 or jiaobaisun 茭白筍 is actually the sheath of the aquatic grass known as Manchurian wild rice (Zizania latifolia, related to American wild rice), that has been infected by the fungus Ustilago esculenta, which is closely related to the corn smut fungus (yet another unappetizing English name). When the thick infected sheaths have been peeled like bamboo shoots, they reveal a firm, plump, creamy-white center "shoot." When stir-fried, this shoot-like food is delectably crisp in texture, refreshingly sweet, and utterly delicious.

20 See the Dried Wild-Rice Shoots recipe in the next chapter ("Side Dishes").

21 Qingcai 青菜 literally means "greenish-blue vegetable" and describes a wide variety of mustard greens (typically Brassica rapa), depending on where you are in China. Terms such as "green Chinese cabbage" or "bok choy" are sometimes used, but since these qingcai plant varieties do not have consistent names in English, the transliteration is used instead.

22 The character nuo 懦 means "weak or timid" and is translated here as being in this case soft and tender. One sees this term used also to describe the textures of foods such as well-stewed pork belly or the flesh of avocados, and it works well for describing well-done mustard stems.

A Note on Identifying Vegetables

Identifying and translating vegetables in *The Way of Eating* can be a challenge. Not only can one Chinese name refer to several vegetables, but the usage of the names often changed over time, or the vegetables themselves may no longer be in (popular) use. For example, *da tou cai* 大頭菜 (lit. big head vegetable) can refer to various mustards of the genus *Brassica*, including kohlrabi, tatsoi, and turnip. The first two are stems, the latter is a root. Although kohlrabi is most common in modern usage, only the stem of tatsoi is native to China. *Da tou cai*, however, can also refer to the mustard used to make hot pickled mustards, called *zhacai* 榨菜 in modern Chinese.

Another example is napa cabbage (*Brassica rapa* subsp. *pekinensis*), which is called *baicai* 白菜 (white vegetable) or *da baicai* 大白菜 (great white vegetable) in modern Chinese. Yuan Mei, however, uses the term *huang yacai* 黃芽菜 (yellow shoot vegetable) when talking about napa cabbage. Both names describe the appearance of the vegetable, referring to its size and color (large and bright milky white), or the heart of cabbage (yellowish, covered by tougher, green-tinged, outer leaves). When he mentions *baicai* 白菜, however, he refers to bok choy.

Finally, perhaps the most confusing group of vegetables is referred to by a variety of names, including *taixincai* 臺心菜, *taicaixin* 臺菜心 or simply *taicai* 臺菜. They refer to a wide range of items, among them seaweed, a variety of mustard greens including *choy sum*, or even celtuce. Added to the mix is cauliflower (*caihuatou* 菜花頭) and Chinese broccoli (*jielan* 芥兰). Based on the circumstances of each individual recipe, the most likely option has been translated. In a few cases, however, the name has been left untranslated, because there isn't enough evidence to positively identify one specific vegetable.

Bok Choy

Bok choy can be stir-fried or braised with bamboo shoots. It can also be braised together with slices of dried-cured ham or chicken broth.

Napa Cabbage

The best specimens of this vegetable come from the north. Prepare it seasoned with vinegar, or braise it with dried shrimp.[23] Serve it

---

23 There is a question of when napa cabbage is supposed to be "done." In the recipe "Braised Ham with Napa Cabbage Hearts" ("Sacrificial Animals" chapter), Yuan Mei indicated that the cabbage should be braised for half a day, so perhaps it is the same here? This classic home-style

immediately when done; any delay changes its color and flavor for the worse.

Tatsoi[24]

Stir-fried tatsoi hearts are best prepared so that they are still crisp and dry without any broth. Specimens harvested from under a blanket of snow are especially tender. Those prepared by the household of Prefect Wang Mengting are the most refined. Do not accompany it with anything. It is best cooked in rendered lard.

Spinach[25]

Spinach is plump and tender and can be prepared by boiling with soy sauce, water, and tofu. In Hangzhou, people know this as "gold inlaid on a slab of white jade." This vegetable is thin but quite meaty and thus does not require cooking with bamboo shoot tips or shiitake.

Mushrooms

Mushrooms are not just for making soup; they are also good when stir-fried. White button mushrooms tend to contain sand and become moldy rather easily, and must be stored and prepared

---

preparation for napa cabbage is known today as *kai yang baicai* 開陽白菜 and involves braising napa cabbage in water or broth for around ten minutes, with ingredients such as shiitake, dried shrimp, dried flounder, or dried ham providing umami. Of all the braised napa cabbage dishes, one of the most famous has to be the mundane-sounding Napa Cabbage in Boiled Water (*kai shui baicai* 開水白菜). When served, this atypical Sichuan dish looks exactly like its name: napa cabbage hearts in a tureen of clear water. This "boiled water," however, is actually an exquisitely prepared consommé as full of umami as a superior Chinese broth (*gao tang* 高湯). Despite its simple appearance, this dish is flamboyantly wasteful and extravagant, leaving a mountain of depleted remains from several chickens, ham, and egg whites, along with a large mound of outer napa cabbage leaves left over from extracting the heart.

24 There are three mustard greens known in Chinese as *piao'ercai* 瓢兒菜: arugula, baby bok choy, and tatsoi (*tacai*塌菜). Yuan Mei gives a clue by saying that the ones from under snow are the most tender. Out of the three, only tatsoi (*Brassica rapa* subsp. *narinosa*) is known to be cold resistant, and can be harvested even after frost..

25 *Bocai* 菠菜, or spinach, literally translates to "Persian vegetable," which points to the trade between the two civilizations in ancient times.

correctly. Shaggy mane mushrooms are easy to prepare and also enjoyable.[26]

Pine Mushrooms

Pine mushroom are the best when stir-fried with white button mushrooms. They are also excellent stir-fried with autumn sauce on their own. Unfortunately, they cannot be kept long, though they work well in dishes, providing them a delicate savoriness. Because of how tender they are, pine mushrooms can also be added to line the bottom of the bowl of the bird's nest.

Three Ways of Preparing Wheat Gluten

Wheat gluten exist in several forms in Chinese cuisine, including fried puffed balloons (*zha mianjin qiu* 炸麵筋球), spongy bread-like (*kao fu* 烤麩), and wrapped sausages (*mianjin chang* 麵筋腸).

For the first method, fry the gluten with oil in a wok until seared and dry, then braise them plain with chicken broth and mushrooms. For the next method, do not sear them but rather boil them in water. Cut into slices and stir-fry with concentrated chicken extract, then add winter bamboo shoots and green onions. The household of examiner Zhang Huaishu prepares this extremely well. When plating, it is more suitable to roughly tear the gluten than slicing them. Stir-fry them with the soaking liquid of dried shrimp and sweet soy sauce for an exceptionally good dish.

Two Ways of Preparing Eggplant

The household of Instructor Wu Xiaogu peels the skin off the eggplants, soaks them in boiling water to rid them of their bitter taste, then sears them in rendered lard. When searing, one must

---

26 White button mushrooms and the shaggy mane mushroom are both great when young, but over time button mushrooms become loose with inky-black gills, while shaggy mane mushrooms turn into a mushy black mess.

wait for the water used for soaking the eggplants to cook dry, then dry-braise them in sweet soy sauce and water. This is exceptionally good. The household of Magistrate Liuba cuts their eggplant into small pieces without peeling the skin, fries them until slightly browned, and then stir-fries with autumn sauce in hot oil for a great dish.

I have learned these two recipes, but I have yet to have success with them. Still, if one steams them until soft, then slices them open, and dresses them with sesame oil and vinegar, one gets a dish well suited for summer eating. Eggplant can also be braised until dry to make jerky and served like that on a dish.

Amaranth

One should choose the tender tips of amaranth and stir-fry them dry. The dish is made even better with the addition of dried shrimp or shelled shrimp. No liquids should be allowed to pool during stir-frying.

Taro Soup

The texture of taro is soft and rich, and is suitable for cooking with strong-flavored meat or simple vegetable dishes. It can be chopped finely and made into a thick duck soup, braised with pork, or braised with tofu, soy sauce, and water. The household of official Xu Zhaohuang chooses small taro and braises them with tender chicken for an incredibly good soup. Sadly, the recipe for this has been lost. On the whole, one uses only seasonings for preparation of this dish and does not use any water.

Tofu Skin

Soak the tofu skin until supple and mix with autumn sauce, vinegar, and dried shrimp to make a dish well suited for summer. The household of Assistant Minister Jiang makes a nice dish by adding sea cucumbers to it. It is also good in a soup with laver and peeled shrimp. It can also be braised with mushrooms and bamboo shoots for a very good clear soup. Cook the tofu skin until soft.

Monk Jing Xiu of Wu Lake rolls the tofu skin into a cylinder, cuts it into segments, lightly browns them in oil, and braises them with mushroom for an excellent dish. Do not add chicken broth.

Lentil Pods[27]

Gather freshly picked lentil pods and stir-fry with pork broth, removing any pork and keeping just the lentils.[28] If one is stir-frying them plain, then it is better to use more oil. Soft and fleshy ones are the best. Those that are coarse and thin were grown in poor soil and should not be eaten.

Calabash and Snake Gourd (Cucumber)

First, stir-fry slices of grass carp, then add the calabash (*Lagenaria siceraria* var. *hispida*) and braise everything together in soy sauce. Prepare cucumber (*Trichosanthes cucumerina*) in the same manner.

Braised Wood Ear and Shiitake

The Dinghui Monastery of Yangzhou knows how to braise wood ear until doubled in thickness, and shiitake until tripled in thickness.[29] Prepare a mushroom broth first to use as the cooking liquid in this recipe.

Winter Melon

There are numerous uses for winter melon. It can be combined with bird's nest, fish, eel, rice eel, and ham. The Dinghui Monastery of Yangzhou prepares it particularly well. Their dish is red as blood amber and cooked without use of strong-tasting *hun* broth.

---

27 Lentil pods (*biandou* 扁豆) can refer either to the slightly poisonous hyacinth bean (*Lablab purpureus*) or lentils (*Lens culinaris*). The former is not commonly consumed, so it is likely the latter, but in pod form; even in modern Chinese cuisine, lentil pods are stir-fried with pork.

28 This is another example of using the meat for its fat and flavor only.

29 One of the more popular agents used for reconstituting meats and dried foods (a process called *fa* 發) in modern Chinese cuisine is baking soda. A pinch added to chicken tenderizes and gives the meat a slight "bounce." Too much, however, gives everything an odd flavor and texture. It makes one wonder what the monks were adding to their soaking liquid to receive such results.

Braised Fresh Water Caltrop[30]

To braise fresh water caltrop, boil them in chicken broth. Before serving, remove half the broth. Only those that were seen harvested from the pond are fresh, and only those that float on the surface of water are tender. Braise them until soft with new chestnuts and ginkgo nuts for an especially good dish. One can also eat them with sugar or as a snack.

Cowpea

Stir-fry cowpea pods (Vigna unguiculata) with pork. When they are about to be served, remove the meat and keep the cowpeas. Use the most tender parts of the pod and pull off any tough fibers.

Three Types of Braised Bamboo Shoots[31]

Braise *tianmu*, winter, and *wenzheng* bamboo shoots in chicken broth. This is known as "soup of three bamboo shoots."

Taro Braised with Bok Choy

Braise the taro until it is very soft, and then add bok choy hearts to cook and season with soy sauce and water. This is the best recipe of all the home-style dishes. Still, one need to choose bok choy that have been freshly picked and are still plump and tender. Once they start turning a dark greenish blue, they have become tough. When they are not recently picked, they tend to become dry and withered.

---

30 The fact that this recipe specifies "fresh" water caltrop fruits (Trapa bicornis) implies that dried ones were also available. The fruits of the water caltrop look so strange and menacing that one of its common English names is "devil pod."

31 Tianmu 天目 (lit. sky eye) bamboo, winter bamboo (Phyllostachys edulis, dongzhu 冬筍), and wenzheng 問政 bamboo shoots from Wenzheng Mountain in Huangshan. Looking at the recipe "Wenzheng Shredded Bamboo Shoots" below, this is probably a dried bamboo shoot.

Fragrant Pearl Beans

Green soybeans harvested in the evenings during August and September are very large and tender, and known also as fragrant pearl beans (*xiangzhu dou* 香珠豆, edamame). Boil them until done and soak them in autumn sauce and *jiu*. They can be served shelled or left in shell, and are fragrant, soft, and are loved by all. Normal beans cannot be eaten this way.

Indian Aster

Choose the tender tips of the Indian aster (*Kalimeris indica*), a wild edible plant foraged by people in the lower Yangtze River Valley, and serve them mixed with bamboo shoots and vinegar. This can be used to rouse one's spleen after eating greasy food.

Yanghua (Willow Leaf) Greens[32]

Yanghua greens are available during March in Nanjing. They are as supple and crisp as spinach. It is a vegetable with a truly elegant name.

Wenzheng Shredded Bamboo Shoots

Wenzheng bamboo shoots are from Hangzhou. Those that are brought in by people from the region are typically in lightly salted and dried form. One must soak them until soft, cut them into shreds, and braise them in a meaty chicken broth. Marshall Gong boils shoots in autumn sauce, bakes them until dry, then serves them thus. The people of Huizhou eat this as a delicacy and are

---

32 *Yanghua* 楊花 (lit. willow flower) is another name for the downy seeds of the weeping willow (*Salix babylonica*). It is unclear, however, what these *yanghua* greens actually were. While there is no information on a vegetable of this name in any other Chinese text, there are traditions in many parts of China of eating the new leaf shoots and flower buds of the willow tree (*liushu ya* 柳树芽) when they open up in the spring around March. Therefore, *yanghua* greens are quite possibly willow leaf sprouts.

enraptured by its flavors.[33] I laugh and cannot wait for them to awaken from their dreams.

Stir-Fried Shaggy Mane Mushrooms

The monks from the great monastery of Wu Lake wash the shaggy mane mushrooms to rid them of sand, then stir-fry them with autumn sauce and *jiu* until done. They plate and serve them to guests at their banquets. This dish is incredibly good.

Radish Cooked in Lard

Stir-fry the radishes in rendered lard, then add dried shrimp and braise them until completely done. When one is about to plate the dish, add chopped green onions. The radishes should be translucent and red like amber.

---

33 This dried bamboo shoot snack is similar to Chinese beef jerky.

Side Dishes and Appetizers

The Chinese term *xiaochi*, often translated as "snack," is actually more like a small and easy-to-prepare meal. Another well-known, but often misunderstood concept is that of dim sum (*dianxin*), which is best understood as an appetizer. These two chapters cover side dishes, mainly noodles and vegetable dishes, as well as dumplings, smaller dishes that can be served as appetizers, and some desserts. China does not have a strong tradition of desserts and sweet treats, and when they do make cakes or candy, often using nuts and dried fruits like dates, they are generally much less sweet than what we are used to in the West.

Side Dishes

Side dishes accompany main dishes, just like petty officers accompany and support the six high imperial officers. All these dishes here awaken the spleen, liven one's appetite, and eliminate waste. The following is the list of side dishes.

Dried Bamboo Shoots

Dried bamboo shoots are produced in many regions, but those baked and dried at home are the best. Choose fresh bamboo shoots and boil them with salt until done, then put them on a basket and bake them dry. One needs to watch them around the clock, since allowing them to bake over a weak flame will cause the preparation to fail. If one uses light soy sauce during preparation, then the color will be a bit dark. This can be prepared using spring and winter bamboo shoots.

Tianmu Bamboo Shoots

Tianmu bamboo shoots are sold wholesale in Suzhou. The ones in the basket close to the lid are the best, but go two inches lower in the basket and one finds shoots with old roots and hard segments. The prices are very high, so buy only the shoots close to the basket lid; if one does this enough times, one will eventually get enough of the good shoots.

Yulan (Jade Orchid) Slices

Bake slices of winter bamboo shoots and marinade with a small amount of honey. The household of Sun Chunyang from Suzhou has salty and sweet forms of this dish, with the salty one being better.

Vegetarian Ham

In Chuzhou [Lishui, Zhejiang Province] dried bamboo shoots are known as "vegetarian ham" and are sold in slices. Their outsides, however, are much too tough. One might as well buy some *mao* bamboo shoots[1] and bake them oneself for better results.

---

1 *Maosun* 毛筍 (*mao* bamboo shoots) literally translates as "coarse" or "hairy" bamboo (*Phyllostachys edulis*).

Dried Bamboo Shoots from Xuancheng

The bamboo shoots from Xuancheng in Anhui Province are dark in color and plump. They are largely similar to *tianmu* bamboo shoots with some subtle differences and are extremely good.

Ginseng Bamboo Shoots

Shape thin bamboo shoots into the form of ginseng, adding a bit of honey water during their preparation. People from Yangzhou value this item highly, which makes them rather expensive.

Bamboo Shoot Sauce

Steam ten *jin* of bamboo shoots for a day and a night. Pierce the segments of the shoots and spread them on a board. In the same manner as making tofu, put another board on top of them and press to squeeze out the juice. Add one *liang* of toasted salt to the juice to make bamboo shoot sauce. One can make dried bamboo shoots from the pressed shoots by sun-drying them. The monks of Tiantai make this to give as gifts.

Wine Lees Sauce[2]

Wine lees sauce is produced in Taicangzhou in Suzhou. The more aged it is, the better.

Shrimp Sauce

Buy many *jin* of shrimp and boil them in a pot with autumn sauce. Remove them from the pot, strain the autumn sauce through cloth and wrap the strained shrimp in the cloth. Place both in a crock to brew.

---

2 In his book, the *Little Guide on Nurturing Life* (*Yangxiaolu* 養小錄), the Qing dynasty author Gu Zhong 顧仲 indicated that wine-lees sauce (*zaoyou* 糟油) is made by mixing unfiltered rice wine with lees, sesame oil, salt, and seasoning. This seems a bit strange, however, as rice wine and oil do not naturally mix, and there are no emulsifiers to help them do so. The modern version is made by ageing a mixture of wine lees, Shaoxing *jiu*, sugar, salt, and osmanthus flowers. Note that there is no sesame oil in the modern version.

La*hu* Sauce[3]

Pound the chili peppers[4] into a paste and steam with sweet sauce. Finely chopped dried shrimp can be mixed into the sauce.

Smoked Roe[5]

Smoked roe has the color and translucency of amber, with those containing lots of oil being the most sought-after. These are from the household of Sun Chunyang in Suzhou, and the fresher they are, the better. When aged, their flavors change for the worse, and the oils they contain spoil.

Pickled Winter Cabbage and Napa Cabbage[6]

Pickled winter cabbage and napa cabbage are delectable when lightly salted but terrible when overly salty. But to preserve the cabbage over a long time, there is no other option but to use salt.

I once tried to pickle a large vat of it and opened it at the end of summer.[7] Although the ones at the top half of the vat smelled rank and their textures were mushy, the ones at the bottom were uncommonly fragrant and alluring, their color white and as translucent as jade. It was truly incredible! Which goes to show, one cannot judge a noble person by their appearance [skin and hair] alone.[8]

---

3 There is no meaningful translation for *lahu*. La*喇* is generally used to express sound, and *hu* 虎 means tiger. Maybe it has something to do with the sounds one makes after tasting it?

4 During the reign of Emperor Qianlong (r. 1735–1796), many sources indicate that the Qin pepper (*qin jiao* 秦椒) mentioned here is actually chili pepper. For example, Yongzheng's *Shandong Instructions* (*Shandong Tongzhi* 山东通志) states that "Qin peppers are red in color, bear seeds, and are quite as spicy as Sichuan peppers".

5 This sounds a lot like Taiwanese *wuyuzi* 烏魚子, better known in English by its Japanese name *karasumi*. It is translucent amber in color, quite oily, and very tasty when fresh. Considering the color of Yuan Mei's smoked roe, he may have been using a similar method, during which the roe is first dry-cured before being smoked.

6 In modern usage, *dongcai* 冬菜 (winter cabbage) is dried pickled Tianjin cabbage, which is quite similar in color and shape to napa cabbage. Both are harvested during early winter and eaten fresh or pickled. Many people translate pickled napa cabbage as "sauerkraut," but these two dishes taste completely different.

7 The end of summer (*sanzhuang* 三伏) are the last six weeks of summer, which are hot and muggy.

8 This is similar to the English idiom "one cannot judge a book by its cover."

Celtuce

There are two ways of eating celtuce. When newly marinated with soy sauce,[9] they are tender, crisp, and loved by all. For the salted and dried item, they can be eaten sliced and are delicate in taste. The less salty item is much sought-after, since the salty ones taste rather terrible.

Xianggan (Fragrant Dried) Greens

Dry the hearts of spring mustard greens (Brassica juncea) in the wind, take their stalks and salt them lightly, then sun-dry. Mix with jiu, sugar, and autumn sauce, then steam. Dry them in the wind and seal in a bottle.

Winter Mustard Greens

Winter mustard greens are also known as "red in snow."[10] One way of preparing them is to pickle them whole, the less salty the better. Another way is to take the stems and dry them in the wind, pound them until pulverized, and pickle them in a bottle. When matured, they taste extremely sweet and delicate added to fish soup. Vinegar could also be judiciously applied to it during cooking as a pungent ingredient[11], which is very good when used in cooking eel or crucian carp.

Spring Mustard Greens

Take the heart of the mustard green, chop well, and pickle in a bottle until mature. They are also known as nuocai.[12]

---

9 Soy-pickled celtuce is still a common way of serving celtuce.

10 "Red in the snow" (xuelihong 雪裡紅) could be an intentional alternation of "stems in the snow" (xuelihong 雪裡蕻). Note that the last characters of each word are homophones: they are written differently but sound the same. Although the latter is more factual, the former sounds more poetic. The species and variety of this mustard green is Brassica juncea var. crispifolia.

11 It is unclear how adding vinegar to this vegetable while cooking would make it more pungent.

12 Nuocai 挪菜 literally means "shifted" or "kneaded vegetable." This is possibly a corruption of another character, also pronounced nuo, meaning "soft" or "tender."

Mustard Green Heads[13]

Slice the roots of the mustard greens and pickle with the rest of the mustard. They are very crisp. They can also be pickled whole, then sun-dried to make a preserved item that is quite amazing.

Sesame Greens

Dry some pickled mustard greens and chop them until extremely fine. Steam them and serve this as a dish known as "sesame greens." They are perfect for the elderly.

Shredded Firm Tofu

Shred good firm tofu into very fine strips and toss with shrimp and autumn sauce.

Wind-Dried Greens

Take the hearts of winter mustard greens and wind dry. Pickle them and afterward squeeze out their salty juices and put them in a small bottle. Seal the bottle with clay and place it inverted over wood ash.[14] When eaten in the summer, they are yellow in color with an odorous fragrance.

Rice Lees Greens

Take some fully pickled wind-dried greens and wrap them with a vegetable leaf. For each wrapped package, cover it with a layer of fragrant rice lees and pack it tightly into a vat. When they are ready to eat, open each package of preserved greens and serve. The rice lees never touch the pickled greens, yet the greens are flavored by the rice lees.

---

13 It quickly becomes clear that this recipe uses mustard greens' roots, bringing up the question why it is not called just that.

14 Due to its caustic chemistry, wood ash is an effective preserving agent, which is likely employed in this case to prevent fungal growth in the clay bottle seal.

Pickled Greens

Wind-dry the hearts of some winter greens and pickle them lightly with salt. Add sugar, vinegar, ground mustard, and the pickling liquid to a jar.[15] One can also add a bit of autumn sauce. This dish is suitable for when one is drunk and full at a banquet, since it awakens the appetite and takes away the effects of alcohol.

Taicai (Cauliflower) Hearts

Take *taicai* hearts harvested at spring and pickle them, squeeze out their salty juices, and store the hearts in a small bottle. Serve them during the summer. When the flowers are wind-dried, they are known as "vegetable flower heads" and can be cooked with pork.

Datoucai (Kohlrabi)

Datoucai are produced in Cheng'en Temple in Nanjing, and the older they are, the better. They show off their savory flavors best when added to meat-containing dishes.

Radishes

Choose a large and thick radish and pickle it in soy sauce for a day or two before serving. They have a lovely sweet and crisp texture. Some experienced nuns know how to make them into items similar to dried-salted fish, cutting them to form a long chain of butterflies around one *zhang* [three meters] in length, connected and fluttering, without any breaks.[16] It is quite a wondrous sight to behold. Cheng'en Temple has radishes for sale that have been pickled in vinegar, with the aged specimens tasting the best.

---

15 Presumably the mustard greens had already been placed in the jar.

16 Although the Chinese statements are somewhat disjointed, the use of the word *jian* 剪 (to cut with a pair of scissors) instead of the word *qie* 切 (to cut with a knife) evokes the image of a long chain of butterflies cut from paper, except that in this case, radishes are used.

Pickled Tofu

Pickled tofu from the General's Temple in Suzhou is very good, dark colored, and savory. There are two types: dried and moist. There is also the kind with shrimp that is quite savory in taste but a bit unappetizing due to its fishy smell. The white pickled tofu of Guangxi is the very best. Treasurer Wang's household also makes a good pickled tofu.

Three Nuts Stir-Fried with Soy Sauce

Peel the walnuts and almonds. The hazelnuts do not need to be peeled. Fry the nuts in oil until they are crunchy, then add soy sauce but do not allow them to become too brown. The amount of soy sauce that needs to be used depends on the amount of other ingredients.

Agar with Soy Sauce

Gelidium amansii is the species of the agar algae. It is red in color and is now harvested mainly for extracting agar, a thickening agent used as a vegetarian alternative to gelatin.

Wash the agar until clean and put it in soy sauce. Rinse the agar when itit is ready to be served. This is also known as "Qilin greens."[17]

Agar Cakes

Simmer the agar until soft and mash into a fine paste. Slice it into pieces with a knife. The color resembles that of beeswax.

Little Pine Mushrooms

Boil the pine mushrooms with soy sauce together in a pot until done. Remove and add them to a jar with sesame oil. They can be eaten after two days; their flavor will change for the worse if they are kept too long.

---

17 The reference to the mythical, unicorn-like creature *qilin* 麒麟 may be due to the bright red, antler-like form of the algae.

Mud Snails[18]

Mud snails (*Bullacta exarata*, mollusk or Korean mud snail) are produced in Xinghua and Taixing (in Jiangsu Province). Use the newly hatched ones, which are most tender. Soak them in fermented rice *jiu*, add sugar, and they will spit out their oil.[19] Although they are known also as "mud conchs," they are best without any mud.

Jellyfish

Use tender jellyfish and soak it in sweet wine for a unique dish. The shiny portion of the jellyfish is known as "white skin," which can be sliced into strips, tossed with *jiu* and vinegar, and served.

Shrimp-Roe Fish

Shrimp-roe fish are produced in Suzhou. When these little fish are born, they already contain tiny roe. When cooked while they are still raw and fresh, and eaten right after, they taste better than any dried fish.

Soy-Pickled Ginger

Take fresh tender ginger and pickle lightly with salt. Marinate first in a coarse-tasting soy sauce, then marinate in a fine-tasting soy sauce.[20] Repeat this three times to complete. An old technique

---

18 This is a well-loved culinary creature lauded in various texts since the Ming dynasty. In his book *Investigation of Flavours from the Sea* (*Haiwei suoyin* 海味索隐), Ming dynasty official and food enthusiast Tu Benjun 屠本畯 devotes a section to it, named "Song of the mud snail" (*Tutie ge* 吐铁歌), that states: "*Tutie* is also known as 'mud snail,' with the best ones coming from the rice paddies of the south. Harvest them during the rainy season of May. The three Wu officials were ones who adored mud snails and stated that regardless of whether they were eating a meal, drinking *jiu*, or having tea, it was always welcome."

19 Perhaps this "oil" is not really a hydrophobic greasy item, but thick slippery mucus?

20 Since *jiang* 醬 generally refers to soy sauce, the differentiation here between "coarse" (*su* 粗) and "fine" (*xi* 細) is puzzling. It could refer to differences in flavor, texture, or thickness. Perhaps the first is simply there to make the ginger salty and leach out some water, while the second gives the ginger a more refined flavor.

Cicada molt shells (*chan tui* 蟬蛻) are used in Traditional Chinese Medicine to reduce inflammation, heal itchy skin, promote clear vision, and control muscle spasms.

adds the molted carapace of the cicada to the marinade, which allows the ginger to be -stored for a long time without becoming tough.

Soy-Pickled Cucumber

Pickle the cucumber with salt, air-dry them, and put them into soy sauce in the same manner as soy-pickled ginger. It is not hard to make pickled cucumbers that are sweet in flavor, but it is hard to make ones that are crisp. The household of Shi Luzhen in Hangzhou makes the best pickled cucumbers. It is said that pickling them in soy sauce, drying, then pickling them in soy sauce again will make the thin skin of the cucumbers wrinkle and crisp in texture when eaten.

Young Fava Beans[21]

Young fava beans are most tender and are remarkable good when stir-fried with pickled mustard greens. It is best to eat them as soon as they have been harvested.

Salted Eggs

Salted eggs from Gaoyou are very good, with deep reddish yolks loaded with oil. This is Master Gao Wenduan's favorite food. At banquets, he would honor his guests by first serving it to them with his own chopsticks.

Place the whole egg on a plate, cut it in half, and serve the shell, yolk, and whites all together. One should not remove the whites

---

21 *Candou* 蠶豆 (here translated as fava beans) literally means "silkworm beans." The origin of this name can be traced back to the Yuan dynasty and comes from the fact that the insides of the large, flat, brown beans resemble mature silkworm pupae. This first record was the *Book of Agricuture* (*Nongshu* 農書) by Wang Zhen 王禎, who stated: "Fava beans get their name from mature silkworm pupae." Interestingly, both fava beans and peas were erroneously lumped together as one item in this manual. The error was only noticed and corrected later by Li Shizhen in his *Compendium of Materia Medica*. This rather obvious error likely hints to when both leguminous plants were introduced into China and information about them was relatively scarce and incomplete.

and reserve only the yolk because the flavors would be incomplete, and the oils from the yolk would leach out.

Huntao[22]

Punch a small hole in the shell of a chicken egg and pour out its white and yolk. Remove the yolk and reserve the white. Mix it with thickened chicken extracts and braising juices. Beat the mixture with chopsticks until it is completely blended, then pour it back into the eggshell. Seal the opening with paper and steam the egg in a rice pot until done. Peel off the shell; it is indistinguishable from any chicken egg, but far more savory in taste.

Dried *Jiaogua* (Wild Rice Stems)[23]

Marinate the *jiaogua* in soy sauce, then let it dry in the wind. Slice it and store it as a dried food item. Use it as one would dried bamboo shoots.

Dried Tofu from Niushuo[24]

Dried tofu manufactured in Niushuo is the best. There are, however, seven sellers of the item in the foothills. Still, those made in the household of the monk Xiaotang are the best of them all.

Soy-Pickled Snake Gourd

When the snake gourd is still small and young, collect the thinner specimens and marinate them in soy sauce. They are crisp and savory sweet.

---

22 The meaning of *huntao* 混套 is unclear. The first character can mean "mixed" or "a mess," while the second could mean "a cover" or "a set." It seems to refer to the fact that the egg is mixed with other ingredients, and then put back in the shell again. Since a good translation is lacking, the transliteration is used.

23 *Jiaogua* 茭瓜 (or *jiao* melon) could refer to either wild rice stems or zucchini. The recipe for *Jiao* (Wild-Rice Stems) in the chapter "Assorted Vegetable Dishes" talks about how to prepare the fresh item; preparation of the dried item is described here.

24 The Niushou Mountains 牛首山 (lit. ox head mountains), low-altitude mountains in Jiangsu Province near Nanjing, are so named because the twin peaks resemble ox horns.

A Note on Appetizers

In English, the term *dian xin* 點心 (lit. touching the heart) is typically trans-literated as dim sum, based on its approximate Cantonese pronunciation *tim sam*. In fact, the Western use of dim sum is limited to the Cantonese tradition of serving many small dishes, known more commonly in Canton-ese as *yum cha* (or tea drinking). It is therefore probably better to translate *dian xin* as "appetizer." The etymology of the term *dian xin* may come from the fulfillment that the food brings, touching the eater's heart, or from the traditional idea that dotting the pupil in the eyes (or "dotting the heart") of human or animal figure in paintings could bring them to life. The quint-essential equivalent of *dian xin* appetizers in the Western tradition would be the little sandwiches eaten with afternoon tea, antipasti, tapas, or hors d'oeuvres.

APPETIZERS

Emperor Zhaoming [Xiao Tong] of the Liang dynasty ate appetizers for small meals. Likewise, aunt Zheng Can advised uncle to "have appetizers." Appetizers certainly have a long history, thus the following is the list of appetizers.

Eel Noodles

Take a large eel and steam it until soft. Pull off its flesh and discard the bones, add it to wheat flour, combine with clear chicken broth, and knead the dough. Roll the dough flat and slice into thin strips, then boil in chicken broth, ham broth, and mushroom broth.

Warm Noodles

Take thin noodles, boil them in broth, strain them, and put them into a bowl. Combine with chicken and concentrated savory shiitake mushroom broth when one is ready to eat. Everybody ladles the sauce on the noodles themselves.

Rice Eel Noodles

Simmer rice eel to make a savory broth. Add noodles to it and boil. This is a Hangzhou recipe.

Skirt Sash Noodles

Take a small knife and cut the dough into broad strips. These are known as "skirt sash noodles." In general, when preparing this noodle dish, it is best when served with a large amount of soup and braising liquids in the bowl so that the noodles cannot be seen. It is much preferable to wait until [the noodles] have been finished before adding more; this way it hooks people in to keep eating. This recipe is very popular in Yangzhou, and quite understandably so.

Vegetarian Noodles

First, simmer the mushrooms for one day to extract their juices and allow them to settle and clarify.[1] The next day, simmer bamboo

---

1 This seemed to be the trick to make vegetarian food appealing before MSG and other taste enhancers: mushrooms, mushrooms, and more mushrooms.

shoots for their juice and boil the noodles in it. This technique comes from the monks of Yangzhou's Dinghui temple, who make it very well but refuse to transmit the recipe to others. One can, however, approximate it to a certain extent. The broth has a pure dark color, and some say shrimp broth has been added secretly. As for the original juice from the mushrooms, simply let the dirt and sand settle and do not change the water. Once the water has been changed, the original flavors would be diluted.

A Note on Cake, Bread, and Pudding

The word *bing* 餅 describes a flour or starch-based, non-wet dough product that is somewhat flattened, and usually disk shaped. It can be translated as (pan)cake, pastry, or even flatbread.

The word *gao* 糕 is used generally to describe a wide range of wet but solid food items, translated variously as cake or pudding. More traditionally, the word refers to a variety of moist, pudding-like dishes made from rice starch that are similar in density and texture to polenta (e.g. radish *gao*, taro *gao*). If made from glutinous rice, imagine a chewier, stickier polenta (e.g. *nian gao*). Still others can be flufier or spongelike, similar to a western pound or sponge cake (e.g. *mala gao*). In this book, we have decided to not rigidly translate the words *bing* and *gao* as either cake or pudding, but rather more dynamically by the manner in which they are used or presented. As such, *bing* and *gao* here may variably be translated as bread, cake, or pudding.

Straw Cape Flatbread[2]

Mix cold water into dry flour, but not too much. Knead the dough and roll it flat, then roll up the flattened dough. Roll it flat again, then spread lard and white sugar evenly on it. Roll the dough up again, then roll it flat into a thin flatbread, and sear in lard until golden brown. If one wants a salty version, one can use green onions, Sichuan pepper, and salt instead.

---

2 This name could come from the loose, flaky, layered texture of the flatbread, which roughly resembles that of the traditional straw cape used as raincoats in East Asia before the introduction of synthetic cloth.

Shrimp Cakes

Combine raw shelled shrimp, green onions, salt, Sichuan pepper, and a small amount of sweet *jiu*. Add water and flour, then sear in sesame oil until done.

Crepes[3]

The household of Provincial Officer [in charge of civil and fiscal matters] Kong of Shandong makes crepes that are thin as cicada wings, as big as a tea dish, and unsurpassed in pliancy, softness, and smoothness. My household tried to replicate this recipe, but the results were not up to par, and we have no idea why it is so.

The people of Qin[4] made small tins out of pewter, each of them holding thirty thin cakes. Each guest was given a tin. The crepes were each as small as the width of tangerines. The tins had lids so they can be stocked and stored.

Fill the crepes with stir-fried shreds of pork, sliced as thin as hairs. The green onions should also be prepared in similar manner. They can also be wrapped with pork and mutton in equal parts, which are known as "Western crepes."[5]

Song Cakes[6]

The Jiaomenfang store at the Lotus Bridge in Nanjing makes the best.

---

3 These are known in Fujianese (Southern Min dialect) as *popiah* (the pronunciation of this word is strongly nazalized) and are rarely referred to using the Mandarin pronunciation *bobing* in Taiwan.

4 People of Qin (*Qinren* 秦人) is used today to describe people from Shanxi Province, but it may not have been used in the same manner during the Qing dynasty.

5 They are called "Western" because of the large Muslim population in the western regions of China, who are, unlike the Han Chinese, major consumers of mutton and lamb. Interestingly, pork is added here, which hints at this being a Sinicized version of a foreign dish. Perhaps something like a Moroccan *warqa* (or *ouarka*)?

6 *Song bing* 松餅 literally means "pine cake." Most likely the use of the "pine" character is a corruption or simplification of *song* 鬆, meaning loose or flaky; thus, the more accurate translation would be "flaky cake." At present, there are cakes in Shanghai known as *gaoqiao songbing* 高橋松餅, or "tall bridge pine cakes," which look remarkably like Taiwanese *ludoupeng* 綠豆碰, (lit. puffed-up

Dough Mice[7]

Mix hot water with flour. Wait for the chicken extract to boil, then use chopsticks to pinch and pick off the dough into pieces of varying size. Add fresh vegetable stems for a unique and flavorsome dish.[8]

Dianbuleng or Meat Jiaozi

Flatten pieces of dough, fill them with pork, then steam them. Making these well is completely dependent on how the filling is prepared. Quite simply, the pork has to be tender, with any tendons removed, and then seasoned well. I've been to Guangdong and ate the *dianbuleng* of Garrison Commander Guan, which were excellent. The filling was made from pork skin that had been braised into a soft paste, which provided a soft and wondrous texture.[9]

Dianbuleng are similar to modern *jiaozi*, or dumplings in English. The oddness of the name *dianbuleng* may imply that it is a Chinese transliteration of the English word *dumpling*. Judging from Yuan Mei's mention of eating them in Guangdong (or Canton, where there were foreigners during Yuan Mei's time), we can assume that these are similar to the dainty southern-style steamed *jiaozi* (*zhengjiao* 蒸餃) rather than their more substantial and thick-skinned northern-style cousins.

Pork Wonton

Wontons are made in the same manner as *jiaozi*.

---

mung bean) and other similar flaky-crust cakes (*subing* 酥餅). If the author did indeed mean this to be a "pine" cake, the most logical interpretation is that it is a cake filled with pine nuts.

7 Perhaps this recipe is named so because the pieces of dough resemble mouse tails. If so, then this would be the rice or starch version of the dish Mice Starch Noodles (*laoshufen* 老鼠粉). This recipe seems to be a coarser version of stick-flicked noodles (*bomian* 撥麵) or stick-flicked little fish (*boyu'er* 撥魚兒). For these noodles, the dough is pulled off into strips using chopsticks and dropped into boiling water.

8 These are the peeled stem from a mustard vegetable (*caixin* 菜心). In this recipe, it probably uses a variety of mustards bred especially for the crisp stem, such as Choy sum.

9 This describes the process of making aspic from pork skin to use as filling, which gives the *jiaozi* a delicious, juicy, unctuous texture and a rich savory flavor. No self-respecting restaurant serving *jiaozi* would skip this step. This may be the first time the technique was recorded in text.

Garlic Chive Pastry

Mix the white portions of garlic chives with pork and add seasonings.[10] Wrap the filling in a flattened piece of dough, and sear in hot oil. Adding butter in the dough makes it all the better.[11]

Dough Cape

Make a dough with sugared water and flour. First heat the wok, then place the dough in using chopsticks, then shape them into the form of a (pan)cake. These are known as "soft wok cakes." This is a Hangzhou recipe.

Grilled Cakes

Pound pine nuts and walnuts until pulverized, mix with crushed rock sugar, lard, and flour.[12] Then grill until both sides are golden brown, with sesame seeds added on top of the dough mixture. Kou'er knows how to make this. The flour must be sifted four or five times, until it is white as snow. Use a two-sided grill, heated by flames on the top and bottom. Adding butter will make this especially good.

Thousand-Layer *Mantou* (Steamed Buns)

The household of Yang Shenrong makes *mantou* that are white as snow, and when pulled apart it looks as if there are a thousand layers. The people of Jinling do not know how to make these. One half

---

10 The bottom white protions of the garlice chives were likely chopped-up before mixing. Modern garlic chive pastries are usually made without meat.

11 The Chinese text could be read as the butter being in the dough or inside the dough wrapper with the filling.

12 Given that this sweet dough is held together by lard, or butter, this is essentially short bread. The use of nuts and sugar in the filling of these grilled cakes is a sign that it is a Near Eastern recipe, making this grilled cake similar to Iranian Qurabiya. Many of these recipes entered China during the Yuan and Ming dynasties and had been recorded by Gao Lian 高濂 in a chapter of his manual *Eight Treatises on the Principles of Life* (*Zunsheng Bajian* 遵生八箋). Culinary descendants of these nuts-based sweets in China can be seen in the peanut and sesame candies popularly consumed.

of the technique comes from Yangzhou, and the other half is from Changzhou and Wuxi.

Miancha (Flour Tea)[13]

Brew a tea from coarse tea leaves and add toasted flour to it. If desired, add sesame paste or milk, too, then add a small pinch of salt. If there is no milk, one can add butter or boiled milk curds.[14]

Making good *mantou* (steamed buns) is much more about technique than the ingredients. First, to make a dough that is gleaming white, it needs to be kneaded until the air bubbles created by the yeast are extremely fine and held fast by well-developed gluten strands. Next, the dough must be correctly flattened and stretched so that it has a fine grain and, once steamed, appears as if the bun consists of many small individual threads.

"Apricot Kernel" Curd

Pound apricot kernels to make a slurry, remove the fiber and residue, and then mix it with rice flour. Add sugar and simmer it.[15]

Fenyi (Starch Cape)[16]

This is made in the same way as *mianyi*. Add sugar and salt together, depending on what is desired.

---

13 *Miancha* (lit. flour tea) is quite similar to the flour-based gruels drunk by the people of northern and western China. The version with butter is similar to Tibetan butter tea mixed with *tsampa* flour. Despite their names, modern *miancha* or *chatang* 茶湯 (tea broth) drinks rarely contain actual tea.

14 *Naipi* 奶皮 (lit. milk skin) is translated here as curds. There are two variations of this product in modern China. The first is the thin skin or membrane that forms on top of boiled milk, which is similar to how tofu skin (*doupi* 豆皮) is produced. The second variation is the thick rubbery residue left on the side of the pot when milk has been boiled. It is unclear which one Yuan Mei is referring to here, but the former may be the more traditional item, also popular among the nomadic people of Central Asia, whose cuisine had a clear influence on many recipes in this chapter.

15 This recipe is more or less similar to the modern dessert known as "almond tofu," except rice flour is used to thicken the "milk" instead of the almond flavoring, gelatin, or agar used nowadays. The milk is made in the same manner as soymilk, in which the kernels are soaked and ground into a pulp, the milky liquid is squeezed out of the pulp, and the milk is then boiled.

16 It is unclear what exactly this recipe, or the *mianyi* mentioned in it, refers to. Perhaps it is related to the Straw Cape Flatbread recipe.

Zongzi (Glutinous Rice Wrapped in Bamboo Leafs)

Take bamboo leaves, fill their insides with white glutinous rice, and boil them. They are small and pointed, just like fresh young water caltrop.

Radish Soup Balls

Finely shred radishes using a grater and boil them to remove their strong odor.[17] Dry slightly, add green onions, and mix with soy sauce. Fill this into balls of starch dough and fry in sesame oil. When the soup boils, it is ready.[18] Imperial prince Chunpu's household makes radish cakes, which my chef Kou'er has learned to make.[19] One can also use the same technique to make garlic chive cakes or pheasant cakes.

Rice Starch Soup Balls

Water-ground rice starch is made by grounding glutinous rice on a wet mill stone. The use of water to lubricate and soften the grains results in an extremely fine-powdered starch. The same technique is not possible with grains such as wheat, because they contain so much gluten that the ground wheat would start to knead itself in a wet grinding.

When one uses rice starch to make soup balls, the resulting items are incredibly smooth and fine. Fill them with a stuffing made of pine nuts, walnuts, rendered lard, and sugar. Likewise, one can also make a filling using tender pork with tendons removed, which has been pounded into a paste and blended with chopped green onions and soy sauce.

17 Modern shredded radish cakes (*luobo si bing* 蘿蔔絲餅) use the same preparation method to get rid of the strong radish odor.

18 The instructions here are rather strange. Either the fried soup balls are added into a pre-made soup, or soup is added to the balls while they are frying (in the manner of Chinese pan-fried dumplings and buns). I believe that the previous sentence, indicating the balls were fried, were meant for the shredded radish in the first sentence. Basically, the radish is prepared, seasoned, and fried before being wrapped in dough; then the balls are boiled until done.

19 Since radish cakes (*loubuo bing* 蘿蔔餅) are mentioned here, it implies that the soup balls are simply the "wet" version of the pan-fried dish.

The method for making rice starch is as follows: soak glutinous rice in water for a day and night, and put it into a watered mill stone to grind, catching the ground rice in a cloth. Put wood ash on the bottom of the cloth to help get rid of the residue.[20] Collect the finely ground starch and sun-dry before use.

Lard Pudding

Mix pure glutinous rice starch with rendered lard and steam it on a plate until done. Rock sugar is also pounded into a powder and added to the starch. When it has finished steaming, cut it open with a knife.

Snowflake Pudding

Steam glutinous rice and pound it into a paste. Use a mixture of crushed sesame and sugar as the filling. Beat it flat and slice into square pieces.

Soft Fragrant Cakes[21]

The best soft fragrant cakes are from Dulin Bridge in Suzhou. The second best are *huqiu* cakes from the household of Xishi. Those from Nanjing's south gate outside Bao'en Temple are the third best.

Hundred Nut Cakes

The ones sold by the person just outside of Beiguan in Hangzhou are the best.[22] The ones made of glutinous rice starch, with lots of pine nuts and walnuts, but without diced candied orange peel are the better kind. Its sweetness comes neither from honey nor

---

20 It is unclear exactly how the wood ash helps with this process of making water-ground starch.

21 There is no record of what exactly these "soft fragrant cakes" were, how they were made, or with what ingredients.

22 Beiguan 北關 was a commercial and cultural district in Hangzhou, at least during the Sui Dynasty. In modern times, it is known for its night market.

sugar, and they can be kept for either short or longer durations. My household could not find the recipe for this.

Starch balls (*fentuan* 粉團) are quite similar to the modern-day green balls (*qingtuan* 青團, or *caozaiguo* 草仔粿) eaten in many parts of China and Taiwan. Vegetable leaves, grasses, or herbs such as Chinese cudweed (*Gnaphalium affine*) or Chinese mugwort (*Artemisia argyi*) are pureed and mixed into rice flour to make a dough, a filling is added, and then this is steamed into a translucent green cake.

Chestnut Cakes

Boil chestnuts until soft, then combine with pure glutinous rice flour and sugar, then steam it to make the cakes. Add melon seeds and pine nuts on top. This is a small dish served during the Chongyang festival.

Green Cakes, Green Balls

Pound and grind green herbs into a juice and mix with starch to make starch balls. The color is like translucent green jade.

Cake of Joyous Unity

Steam acake as one would do with rice. Use a wooden mold and form it into the shape of a small precious stone disk.[23] Grill it on an iron rack using a small amount of oil so that it does not stick to the rack.

Chickpea Pudding

Grind chickpeas until completely pulverized and use the fine flour to make a pudding. Steam it on a plate. When it is time to serve, cut it into slices with a small knife.[24]

---

23 These flat, circular, polished, precious stone disks with a hole in the center (*bi* 璧) have been found in Chinese culture since Neolithic periods.

24 This sounds like the chickpea-based Burmese "tofu," which is made in a similar way, cooking chickpea flour with water to a thick paste and letting it set to the consistency of tofu before cutting it in small pieces.

Chickpea Congee

Grind chickpeas and make it into a congee. Fresh chickpeas give the best results, but one can also make it using older chickpeas. One can add mountain yam or *fuling* for an even better congee.

Fuling, the large fleshy sclerotium of the fungus *Wolfiporia extensa*, is commonly used in Traditional Chinese Medicine and occasionally in Chinese pastries.

Golden Balls

The golden balls from Hangzhou are made from starch and pressed into carved wooden molds to give them the shape of peaches, apricots, and precious metal ingots. The fillings can be either meat or vegetarian.

Lotus Root Starch and Lily Starch

The purity and authenticity of lotus root starch that one has not ground themselves cannot be trusted. This is also true for lily starch.

Sesame Balls

Pound steamed glutinous rice into a paste and form it into balls. Use ground sesame mixed with sugar for the filling.[25]

Taro Starch Balls

Grind taro to make starch and dry it. Use it mixed with rice flour.[26] The Daoists at Chaotian Temple make taro starch balls filled with pheasant that are very good.

---

25 Modern sesame balls (*matuan* 麻圍, also known as *jiandui* 煎堆) are deep-fried and slightly different in that their outsides are coated with sesame seeds while their fillings are not always sesame-based.

26 Left unfilled, these sound like Taiwanese taro balls (*yuyuan* 芋圓) or taro dates (*yuzao* 芋棗).

Cooked Lotus Root

Lotus "roots" are actually rhizomes or underground stems of the sacred lotus (*Nelumbo nucifera*). While it would be more accurate to call them lotus rhizomes, the name "lotus roots" is well established in Chinese cookbooks.

Fill a lotus root with rice and sugar, then boil it by itself. This makes an excellent soup. The roots sold by outside merchants tend to be made with alkaline water,[27] which changes the taste and makes them inedible.

I have always loved eating young lotus roots. Even when they are cooked soft, you can sink your teeth into them and all their natural flavors still remain. If old lotus roots were cooked soft as mud, they would have lost all flavor.

New Chestnuts and New Water Caltrop

When boiled until soft, newly harvested chestnuts have the aroma of shelled pine nuts. The chefs, however, refuse to braise them until soft, so the people of Jinling never know of such flavors, even to the ends of their lives. This is the same for new water caltrops. The people of Jinling prefer eating these in the traditional way.

Lotus Seeds

Although seeds from the *jian* lotus are more expensive, they are not easy to cook like those from the lake lotus. When they are somewhat done, remove their hearts and skin, put them in soup, and braise them over a gentle flame, simmering with the lid closed. Do

---

27 *Huishui* 灰水 can be interpreted in two ways: either as "gray water" or "ash water." The former would imply dirty water, which I would translate as "filthy water." The latter and the more likely meaning is that "alkaline water," in this case a high pH solution containing potassium or sodium hydroxide, was made from wood ash, and the lotus roots were cooked in them. This practice is still done, especially if the lotus roots are old and tough, but it removes the flavors one expects from lotus root. This idea is similar to people adding a pinch of baking soda when cooking split pea soup from old split peas. In this case, the baking soda ($NaHCO_3$) is transformed into sodium carbonate ($NaCO_3$) via thermodecomposition, which actually softens the peas.

not open the lid to look inside while cooking, and do not stop the flame. Do this for a period of two incense sticks [two hours] and the lotus seeds will be done and will be neither raw nor hard.

Taro

On a clear day during the eleventh month [end of November], harvest taro roots and let them dry under the sun until they are quite dry. Place them in straw to prevent them from frost damage. Cook them in spring, and they will have a natural sweetness to them. Commoners do not know of this.

Xiao the Beauty's Appetizer

Just outside the southern gate of Yizhen, a beauty by the name of Xiao makes small appetizers such as *mantou*, cakes, and *jiaozi*. They are small, delicate, adorable, and bright white like snow.

Imperial Scholar Liu's Mooncake

Use flying flour from Dongshan to make a flaky oil pastry crust. Grind pine nuts, walnuts, and melon seeds into a fine powder and add small amounts of rock sugar and lard to make the filling. When eaten, it does not taste excessively sweet, and is also fragrant, flaky, soft, and rich—something truly extraordinary.

Flying flour likely indicates very finely milled wheat flour, similar to our modern-day white wheat flour.

Imperial Scholar Tao's Appetizers of "Ten Sights"

Every New Year's Day, the wife of the imperial scholar Tao will make ten types of appetizers, all using Dongshan "flying flour." They are of strange shapes and cunning forms with multiple swirls of marbled color. When eaten, they are all so sweet and delicious that one is completely overwhelmed by how wonderful they are. Chief

Marshall Sa said, "Try Imperial scholar Kong's thin cakes, and all other thin cakes under the heavens might as well be discarded. Try imperial scholar Tao's "ten sights" appetizers, and all other appetizers under the heavens might as well be discarded." Since Imperial Price Tao's death, this appetizer has become lost like the tune "Scattering of Guangling District."[28] Oh, woe!

Yang Zhongcheng's Western Cakes[29]

In a bowl, blend egg whites with flying flour into a batter. Hammer out a set of copper clamps, with its head patterned and shaped for a cake about the size of a saucer. The inner faces of the top and bottom parts of the clamps should be not more than three millimeters apart.[30] Start a strong flame and heat the copper clamps, ladle on the batter, spread, clamp, and sear. In an instant, the cake is finished. It is as white as snow and translucent like cotton paper. Add a small amount of rock sugar and chopped pine nuts.

White Cloud Crisps

Guoba 鍋巴 or pot adherent is formed from rice that has stuck to the bottom of the pot during the cooking process. These are scraped off and eaten as a snack and sometimes served as a delicacy.

Guoba [pot adherents] from Nanshu are thin as cotton paper and, when fried in oil and dusted with a little sugar, are incredibly crisp. The people from Jinling excel at making these, and call them "white cloud crisps."

---

28 "Scattering of Guangling District" (*Guangling san*) was a musical work from the Eastern Han dynasty written for the *guqin* (a seven-string plucked zither-like instrument). It was lost due to the death of the musician and composer.

29 The term "Western" (*xiyang* 西洋, lit. "Western ocean"), alludes to the overseas (European) origins of this pastry. These cakes are very much like the light wafers eaten throughout Europe as sacramental wafers at communion, as a snack, or sandwiched with jam.

30 These instructions basically explain how to make a clamp-like wafer iron used to make wafer biscuits.

Fengxiao (Wind Thins)

Soak rice starch completely through, form it into small flakes and fry them in rendered lard. When they have been taken out of the pan, immediately sprinkle with sugar. It is as white as frost and melts in the mouth. People from Hangzhou know them as *fengxiao*.

Three-Layered Jade Sash Cakes

Use pure glutinous rice flour to make these cakes, split into three separate layers: one with rice flour, one with rendered lard, and one with white sugar, then sandwich and steam.[31] When it is done steaming, cut it open. This is a recipe from the people of Suzhou.

Transport Officer's Cake[32]

Lu Yayu worked as the transport official until he was rather old. A Yangzhou store made a cake and gifted it to him. So much did he sing its praises, that since then it was given the name Transport Officer's Cake. The color is as white as snow, spotted with rouge that is as red as peach blossoms.[33] Its filling consisted of a small quantity of sugar, and was mild but delectable. The store just outside the office of the transportation officer is the best. Other stores make them out of coarse flour and use poor coloring.

Sand Cakes

Steam glutinous rice flour to make cakes, sandwiching ground sesame and granulated sugar inside.[34]

---

31 It is difficult to imagine how the layers with lard and sugar would hold together without melting into a mess. The part that tells us to "sandwich" it may indicate a last layer consisting of rice flour, but it is unclear from this description.

32 The transport officer (*yunsi* 運司) was an official in charge of general transportation of goods or a position that had oversight on the transport and delivery of salt.

33 Decorating cakes (*gao* and *bing*) with spots of red food coloring is still the norm in China.

34 This recipe describes something quite similar to Singaporean *Kueh tutu*, a snack made of steamed rice flour with a sweet (sugar) filling. The texture is likely similar to the Snowy Steamed Cakes mentioned below.

Little *Mantou* and Little Wonton

Longans (*longyan* 龍眼, lit. dragon eyes) are the sweet fruits of the tropical tree *Dimocarpus longan*. Longan fruits are similar in texture to the better-known lychee, but their taste is slightly more tart and refreshing, with a hint of brown sugar.

Make *mantou* the size of walnuts and serve them directly from the steamer. A pair of them can be picked up with chopsticks. These items are from Yangzhou, where the skill for leavening dough is the best. When one pushes down on the *mantou*, the flattened dough does not exceed half an inch, and when one lets go, it swells back to its original height.

Little wontons should be made as small as longans and cooked in chicken broth.

Snowy Steamed Cakes

When grinding rice for fine flour, use two parts of glutinous rice and eight parts of plain rice, as is typical. Mix the flours together and place it directly onto a plate, and sprinkle it with cool water until it can be readily formed into balls or separated into crumbs. Sieve it through a coarse hemp sieve; any pieces left over should be broken apart and re-sieved until all of the damp flour has been sieved. Combine all the batches of sieved flour evenly so that it is neither too dry nor wet. Cover

Foreign sugar (*yang tang* 洋糖) refers to processed sugar imported from overseas. In the Chinese novel *Dream of the Red Chamber*, there is a reference to *xuehua yang tang* 雪花洋糖 (snow flower foreign sugar) also referring to white sugar from the West.

with a towel and avoid letting it be dried by the wind or sun so it is ready for use. Add foreign sugar to the water so the cake will have even more flavor; mix the rice flour in the way *zhen'er* cake[35] from the city is made.

Take a pewter mold hoop and disk, then wash and scrap them well until very clean. When ready to use, wipe the mold with a cloth using a mix of water and sesame oil. After every steaming, it

---

35 *Zhen'er* 枕兒 literally means "pillow child," which rather mystifies what a *zhen'er* cake actually is.

has to be washed and wiped again. In the pewter hoop, place the pewter disk snugly, and first fill less than half of the mold loosely with the sieved rice flour, lightly place the fruit filling in the center, then loosely fill the mold to the top with more sieved rice flour. Lightly agitate the mold until the contents are flat, set it over the water flask, and cover with the lid. It is ready when one sees the steam shooting out from the opening in the lid. Take the mold out and invert it, first removing the mold hoop and then the disk, and then decorate with rouge.[36] One can use two hoops, filling and steaming them in turn.

The water flask should be washed very clean, filling it with water up to the shoulder of the flask. With prolonged boiling, the water can easily dry up; thus one must observe carefully and refill with hot water as frequently as required.

Preparing Flaky Cakes[37]

Prepare a bowl of cold solid lard and a bowl of boiled water, then mix the lard with the water until smooth. Next, add raw flour and knead thoroughly until soft, in the manner similar to *ganbing*. For the outside [of the cakes], use steamed cooked dough and add lard to it. Combine but don't allow it to become hard.

Next, divide the raw dough into balls the size of walnuts, and divide the cooked dough into balls. Make each a bit small. Wrap the balls of cooked dough into the balls of raw dough and flatten it with a rolling pin into a long cake, eight inches in length and two or three inches in width. Next fold and layer it into the form of a bowl, and then fill them with desired fillings.

---

36 This recipe is a version of the modern red bean cakes (*chidou songgao* 赤豆鬆糕), which consists of coarsely ground rice flour embedded with jujubes, red azuki beans, and sweet red bean paste. It is said to have been the favorite dessert of Soong Mei-ling 宋美齡, the wife of statesman and former president of Taiwan, Chiang Kai-shek. In this older version, the fuit filling (*guoxian* 果餡) could also use jujube fruit, but could even contain nuts such as walnuts or hazelnuts. The mentioned water flask is likely a steaming container.

37 Yuan Mei's description of this recipe is hopelessly confusing. It is almost as if he only *heard* how it is made instead of actually seeing and understanding it. The recipe mentions *shengmian* (raw dough or flour) and *shoumian* (cooked dough or flour), but *mian* can mean both dough *and* flour, adding to the confusion. If understood as dough, raw (or uncooked) dough is made with cold water, while cooked dough is made with boiling water.

Natural Cakes

In Jingyang, the household of Imperial Prince Zhang Hetang makes natural cakes. They use the highest grade white "flying flour," adding a small amount of sugar and lard for crispness, then pull it into the form of a cake in any way desired; it should be about the size of a bowl, neither square nor circular, with a thickness of around six millimeters. Bake the cake over small pebbles the size and smoothness of goose eggs, and it will take on the bumps and creases naturally.[38] When it is golden in color, remove it from the stones. They are incredibly tender and delicious. One can also add salt to them.

Lace-Patterned Mooncake

The household of the Prefect makes a lace-patterned mooncake that is on par with that of Shandong's Imperial Scholar Liu. I have invited his female chef several times to the garden by palanquin to make them. I saw flying flour mixed with raw lard, gathered into balls a thousand times and kneaded a hundred times. The flesh of the jujube fruit was then pushed into the dough as filling, and they were formed to [a mass] the size of a bowl. Each of them was than grasped in one's hands in a manner such that the four sides of the mooncake has scalloped edges in a water caltrop pattern. Take two firepots, and bake them on both top and bottom sides.

The jujubes should not be peeled so that their delicate flavors are retained. The lard should not be rendered so it tastes fresher. When the mooncake is placed in the mouth, it melts away. It is sweet without being greasy and tender without being dry and hard to swallow. At the end, it all depends on the kneading technique of the dough; the more it is kneaded, the better the mooncake will turn out.

Preparing *Mantou*

By chance, I had the opportunity to try the *mantou* of the District Magistrate Long. They were white and fine as snow, and their

---

38 This is almost like the Persian flatbread called *sangak*, which is baked the same way.

surfaces shone bright as silver. I thought this was because the flour was from the north. To this, Long said, "Not true, there is no such thing as northern versus southern flour, all that is required is to mill it extremely finely. When it has been milled and sieved five times, it will naturally become fine and white, there is no need for northern flour."

I have invited their chef to come teach us how to make them, but even after learning how, we still could not get them to be as fluffy and light.

Zongzi of Yangzhou's Hong Residence

The Hong official residence makes *zongzi* by choosing the highest grade glutinous rice, picking out only the grains that are whole, long, and white, and discarding all grains that have split or become broken. The grains are rinsed and swirled until they have absorbed their fill of water, then they are wrapped in a leaf of the large leaf bamboo (*Indocalamus longiauritus*). A large chunk of good ham is placed in the center. Seal them in a pot, cover, and braise them for a day and a night, fueling it with firewood without interruption. When eaten, they are smooth and rich, warm and tender, with the meat melting into the rice. There is another technique: namely, take a fat ham, chop it finely into bits, and mix it directly into the rice.

The Foundation of a Meal

Traditionally, rice has been the staple food in South China, while noodles and grains were more common in the North. Yuan Mei identifies rice as the carrier of all other flavors, the very basic necessity for a successful meal, but even the flavor of rice itself is highly regarded by him, as he writes "the sweetness of rice is superior to a hundred other flavors."

Staple Food

Rice and Congee

Congee and rice are the foundations of a meal, and all accompanying dishes are extras. And it is only through solid knowledge of the fundamentals that one can begin to walk the Way.[1] The following is the list of rice and congee recipes.

---

1 This is a reference to a line from the *Analects of Confucius*: "A noble person directs his efforts to the fundamentals, only once these fundamental have been established can one walk the Way."

Rice

[The Han dynasty statesman] Wang Mang stated, "Salt is the commander of hundreds of meat and fish dishes." I would say, "Rice is the foundation of hundreds of flavors." The *Classic of Poetry* said, "When washing rice it rustles and rustles. While steaming, it gurgles and gurgles." This shows that the ancients also ate steamed rice and were critical of rice that had not been permeated by its cooking liquid. For a person who is good at cooking rice, regardless of whether they are boiling or steaming rice, they are still able to cook it so that each grain remains distinct and has a texture that is soft yet dense as one chews.[2]

There are four keys to making rice: First, one must use good rice, such as fragrant rice, winter's frost, late rice, Bodhisattva rice, or peach blossom rice. Rice ripens in the spring, so on humid days it must be spread out to dry, otherwise one risks it becoming moldy and sickly. Next, one must also rinse the rice well and not skimp on effort when doing so. Rub the rice with one's hands while rinsing it in a sieve and let the water flow through it. Rinse until the water flows clear, without any color from the rice.[3] One must also know how to control the fire, starting first with an aggressive flame and following with a gentle flame. It is best to let rice finish by leaving it to rest, covered, over very low heat. Finally, one must determine the amount of water to use according to the quantity of rice, with neither too little nor too much water; just the right dryness and dampness.

One frequently sees wealthy families who are quite discerning over the quality of their dishes but not their rice. In pursuing trifles and forgetting their foundations, they are quite worthy of ridicule. I do not enjoy ladling soup over rice, since it robs the rice of its original flavors. If there is good soup, one rather should take a mouthful of soup then a mouthful of rice separately, eating one after the other to enjoy the best of both items. If I must do so, I

---

2 When going to a Chinese restaurant, one can tell what the proprietor thinks about the customers and the establishment by which kind of rice they serve: either distinct grains, soft, sweet, and al dente or the mush and paste most places end up serving.

3 The rinsing liquid must be completely clear. Even the slightest cloudy residue, indicative of excess starch dust in the rice, could keep the grains from being distinct and shiny after cooking.

A Note on Rice

Some of the rice varieties mentioned in the text are easier to identify than others, but in general it is not possible to conclusively trace any of them to specific modern varieties. "Fragrant rice" (*xiangdao* 香稻), was recorded in the poetry collection of Tang poet Du Fu 杜甫, the *Quxing Bashou* 秋興八首 in which he wrote: "Each grain of the fragrant rice, kissed by the parrot. That branch on the emerald parasol tree, perched bare by the phoenix." 香稻啄餘鸚鵡粒，碧梧棲老鳳凰枝. This line points to the rarity and preciousness of the rice. "Winter's frost" (*dongshuang* 冬霜), has little or no references in other works. Its name, however, could allude to either the rice's translucent white grains, like that of winter frost, or that the rice is grown and harvested late in the season, when frost is starting to appear. "Late rice" (*wanmi* 晚米), is known to be of higher quality than rice harvested earlier in the season. In fact, it is noted in the Ming dynasty *Compendium of Materia Medica* (compiled by Li Shizhen 李時珍) in the chapter on grains (*gu* 穀) that "for short-grained, non-glutinous rice, white late-ripening rice is the best, and early ripening rice is well below the standard. The rice balances the five organs, is nourishing and beneficial for the stomach's *qi*, and unparalleled in its effectiveness" "粳以白晚米為第一，早熟米不及也。平和五臟，補益胃氣，其功莫逮。"

Xian 秈 rice is a long-grain rice of the Indica variety, such as jasmine or basmati that tends to be less sticky and becomes more fragrant when aged. This contrasts with *jing* 粳 rice, known collectively as the *Japonica* variety, that is sticky like the rice used for sushi. *Xian* rice owes its character to high amylose starch content, while *jing* rice has a much higher amylopectin starch content. The Bodhisattva *xian* rice (*Guanyin xian* 觀音秈) does not appear to be mentioned in contemporary works, which might imply that it is a less common name for a different variety of rice. "Peach blossom *xian* rice" (*tiaohua xian* 桃花秈) is also not found in other texts. Nevertheless, there is another rice with a similar name, "peach blossom rice" (*tiaohua mi* 桃花米) that has been lauded in Chinese cuisines since the Song dynasty. While it is tempting to conflate this with the rice that Yuan Mei mentions, this should be avoided since it is of the *Japonica* variety and would be quite different from the *Indica* variety that Yuan Mei indicated. If, however, the price of today's peach blossom rice is any indication of how expensive Yuan Mei's peach blossom xian rice actually was, it would be anywhere between five to twenty times the price of regular rice.

would rather pour on tea or hot water, which would not deprive the rice of its true flavors.[4] The sweetness of rice is superior to a hundred other flavors. When a connoisseur is served good rice, they can appreciate it without needing any dishes on the side.

Congee

If one sees water but no rice, it is not congee. If one sees rice but no water, it is not congee. The water and rice must meld harmoniously together as one, in softness and richness, before it can be called congee. Master Yin Wenduan stated, "It is preferable that people wait for congee then letting congee wait for them." There is much truth to this well-known statement, since letting it sit too long would cause its flavor to change and its liquids to dry off. Recently there have been people making duck congee by adding pungent meats, or making "eight treasure" congee by adding fruits and nuts, all of which causes the congee to lose its proper flavor. If one really must do so, add mung beans in the summer and millet in the winter. By matching one of the five grains with another and combining things inside the same category, one avoids harming the congee.

I have eaten at the house of a certain inspector, who served several dishes that were fine, but the rice and congee were so coarse and unrefined that I had to force myself to swallow. When I returned home I became violently ill. I joke with others that "such misfortune was brought on by the violent wrath of the gods in my five organs thus there was nothing I could do to prevent it."[5]

In Traditional Chinese Medicine the five organs (*wuzang* 五臟) include the heart, lung, liver, kidneys, and intestines. Owing to their importance, they are also commonly known as the "five-organ temple." So when someone tells you they will be doing some "worshipping at the *wuzang* temple," they're telling you they will be feasting (eating and drinking).

---

4 This resembles *ochazuke*, a Japanese dish where green tea or hot water is poured over rice, usually with savory toppings.

5 Yuan Mei does not want to overtly look like a finicky and unappreciative guest, yet in his opinion the food was really terrible. He uses the explanation of the spirits as an excuse for both himself and the host, as though it was nobody's fault.

A Note on Grain

The five cardinal grains and seeds are of critical nutritional and cultural importance to the Chinese. The list varies from source to source, but typically includes soybeans (*shu* 菽), wheat (*mai* 麦), broomcorn (*shu* 黍), foxtail millet (*ji* 稷), and either rice (*dao* 稻) or hemp (*ma* 麻). Occasionally, the term "six cardinal grains" (*liu gu* 六穀) is invoked, which contains both the latter rice *and* hemp. In this context Yuan Mei is most likely using the term "five grains" to refer collectively to all cereals, pulses, and certain oilseeds.

Liquid Delicacies

This chapter is divided into two sections: one for tea, and one for what can be translated as alcoholic beverages. In this text, it has been transliterated as *jiu*, as explained in the note on page xxx. In the opening lines to this chapter, Yuan Mei mentions the power of alcohol (making people "manic like the wind"), as well as the importance of the "six clears." These six "clears" refer to the beverages mentioned in the classic *Rites of Zhou*, including clear water (*shui* 水), clear *jiu* (*jiang* 漿), unfiltered *jiu* (*li* 醴), roasted rice tea (*liang* 涼), medicinal *jiu* (*yi* 醫), and diluted congee (*yi* 酏). Yuan Mei uses this reference to indicate that one cannot avoid talking about the important drinks.

That said, and as he points out several times, he despised guests who would get drunk before or during a meal, claiming they would never be able to properly taste and appreciate the food, and the efforts of the chef would be wasted.

In Chinese, the term *baijiu* 白酒 or "white liquor" is commonly used to refer to distilled grain liquor, alluding to its colorless clarity—which contrasts with *huangjiu*, or "yellow liquor," which is a brewed, un-distilled alcoholic beverage with a color ranging from light to dark brown. One example of those "yellow liquors" is Shaoxing *jiu*, in the West better known as Shaoxing wine and now primarily used for cooking.

Like the alcoholic drinks, the teas are generally named for their city or region of origin. Elements such as the quality of water and air, geographical location, and climate played a major role on the flavors of the end product. In a country as vast and diverse as China, one can only imagine the range of teas and alcoholic beverages that were (and still are) available.

Tea and *Jiu*

After seven bowls a person becomes manic like the wind. Even after just one cup they would not have a care in the world. One cannot avoid mentioning the "six clears [drinks]." The following is the list of tea and *jiu* recipes.

Tea

If one wants to make good tea, one must first store good water. One should insist on storing water from the Zhongleng or Hui Spring.[1] But how is a typical household supposed to do this? In any case, rain and snow water can be collected and stored. Newly collected water has a harsh flavor, but aged water has a sweet flavor. Having sampled all the teas under heaven, the one from the peaks of Yiwu Mountain that turn pale and white when steeped is the best. This tea, however, is hard to come by since it is a tribute item for the emperor, so what is a commoner to do? Sitting in second place, there is no tea better than Longjing tea. The ones harvested before the Qingming festival [Tomb-Sweeping Day] are known as "lotus hearts," which have such light flavor that it is best to use more when brewing. The ones before the rains are the best, with each grain of tea containing a leaf and a bud, green as jade.[2] The way to store them is to use small paper bags, filling each with four *liang* of tea, and then placing them in a vessel containing quicklime. After ten days, refresh the quicklime, then seal the vessel tightly with paper; otherwise the vapors will leak out, and the colors and flavors of the tea will change for the worse.[3] Boil the water over an aggressive flame, using a hollow centered jar.[4] Brew

---

1 Zhonglengquan and Huiquan are famous springs around Yuan Mei's home, known as the "best" and "second best" springs under the heavens.

2 Tea picked from before the spring rains is known to have more concentrated and complex flavors. Afterward it tends to be more diluted. This is similar to not watering tomatoes a day or two before harvesting, which makes their flavor more intense.

3 Yuan Mei is describing the exact same technique for removing humidity in food still used today. Indeed, quicklime, or calcium oxide (CaO), is one of the common materials used inside the white Tyvek "Do Not Eat" packs in packaged and prepared dried foods. Although silica gel is nowadays more commonly employed as a desiccant for food, quicklime is still used since it is more economical and effective, especially in environments with high humidity. Even though silica gel is safer for humans, tea leaves are often still kept dry using quicklime, albeit packed in safer and more resistant packaging. The first storage with quicklime in this recipe removes any residual humidity in the tea itself, while the change of quicklime is what is used to keep the air in the vessel dry.

4 A hollow-centered jar (*chuanxin guan* 穿心罐) is likely a jar with a chimney in its center, like that found in classic hot pots and Yunnan steam bowls. Some modern tea makers also boil water for tea in a teapot known as a *chuanxin diao* 穿心銚. This looks like a typical clay teakettle but with a chimney going from the bottom of the vessel to either its top or side. The benefit of using such a vessel for boiling water is the increased surface area, which rapidly heats up the water and reduces the time the water degasses before it is at the right temperature and helps improve the taste of the tea.

the tea immediately when the water boils.⁵ If one boils it for too long, the flavors will change. If one waits until after the water has boiled, then the tea leaves will float on the surface. Once the tea is brewed, it should be drunk immediately; if one covers it with a lid, the flavors will again change for the worse. These instructions must be followed exactly, without a hair's width of deviation.

Upon tasting my tea, Pei Zhongcheng of Shanxi said to others, "Yesterday I went by the Sui garden and finally had a cup of good tea." Oh woe is the state of tea making that even a person of stature from Shanxi says this! I have seen Doctor Shi, who grew up in Hangzhou, drink a simmered tea brew that is as bitter as medicine and red as blood upon entering the court. This is no better than those fat-bellied dull-witted individuals who chew betel nuts.⁶ Such vulgarity! Other than the Longjing from the place of my birth, I would rate all other teas far beneath.

Yiwu Tea

I used to dislike tea from Yiwu and found it thick and bitter, as if one were drinking medicine. In the autumn in the year of *bingwu* [1786]⁷, however, I was vacationing at Yiwu and touring Manting Peak to visit several temples. The monks and Daoists there fought to offer me tea.⁸ Their cups were as small as walnuts. The teapots

---

5 The is probably not a full rolling boil (100°C), but a lower-temperature boil like that described in Lu Yu's famous Tang dynasty treatise *Classic of Tea*.

6 It is interesting to note that betel-nut chewing, despite being popular, was already considered a rather lowly and repulsive habit. No doubt this statement was also aimed at Doctor Shi.

7 In ancient China, time (years) was measured using a sixty-year cycle called the Stems-and-Branches (or Chinese sexagenary cycle) system. Each "year" had a two-syllable name, one referring to a heavenly stem, the other an earthly branch. In this case, Yuan Mei refers to the autumn of a *bingwu* year, of which he had two during his lifetime, 1726 and 1786. Given that he likely didn't visit Mt. Yiwu as a ten-year-old boy, he probably meant 1786. This means that Yuan Mei was around seventy years old when he understood the point of Yiwu tea.

8 This statements reminded me of the story of Zheng Xie 鄭燮, a contemporary of Yuan Mei, who rose from poverty to be an Imperial magistrate, only to quit and live as a painter and poet. Once, while visiting a temple in the mountains of Jiangsu, Zheng was received by the head monk why curtly offered him to sit (*zuo* 坐) and ordered him tea (*cha* 茶). After speaking with Zheng and realizing he was not just some commoner, the monk invited Zheng into the temple hall where he politely offered him a seat (*shang zuo* 上坐) and ordered tea to be brought (*shang cha* 上茶). When the monk finally realized that Zheng was a person of fame, Zheng was brought into the monk's formal receiving room and fawningly offered a seat (*qing shang zuo* 請上坐) and good quality tea was ordered to be brought for him (*shang hao cha* 上好茶). Prior to Zheng's departure, the monk asked if

The citron (*Citrus medica*) is a highly fragrant citrus fruit with a thick rind. It is commonly found as candied fruit in Western confections.

were small like citron, with each holding no more than a *liang* of tea. When drinking it, I held back and did not immediately swallow, but breathed in its fragrance, then tasted its flavors and, in this way, savored, meditated, and dwelled on the experience. Indeed, its pure refreshing fragrance wafted up my nose and left a sweet aftertaste on my tongue. After the first cup, I went for one or two more, which left me completely relaxed and at peace, bathed in joy and contentment. From this, I started to feel that Longjing, although delicate and refreshing, is rather thin in taste, and that Yangxian, although pleasant, still lacks charm. Nevertheless, it is rather like comparing jade to crystal, each desirable for different traits. Yiwu is praised and renowned throughout the world, and indeed it fully deserves it without modesty. The tea can be steeped three times without any depletion in its flavor.

Longjing Tea

The mountain teas of Hangzhou are all delicate and refreshing, but the ones from Longjing are the most famous. Each time I return to my place of birth to visit the family tombs, upon meeting the grave keeper we would be served a cup of tea that is clear as water with the greenness of the tea leaves. It is something that even the wealthy could not hope to savor.

Changzhou *Yangxian* Tea

Yangxian tea has the deep color of green jade and the shape of sparrow tongues, and looks like large grains of rice. Its flavor is similar to Longjing, but slightly stronger.

---

his esteemed guest would write him a few lines of poetry as a souvenir to his visit. Much to the embarrassment of the monk, Zheng wrote him the following couplet:

Sit, Take a Seat, Please Do Take a Seat.
Tea, Bring Tea, Bring Good Tea.

Jun Mountain Tea from Dongting

The tea produced in Dongting's Jun Mountain [island] has the color and flavors similar to Longjing, however, the leaves are slightly broader, much greener, and the quantities plucked are very low. Military console Fang Yuzhou once conferred me two jars of it, which were incredibly good. Afterward, others have given me this tea as gifts, but they were all not the real thing from Jun Mountain.

Other teas such as Liu'an, Yinzhen, Maojian, Meipian, and Anhua could be more or less dismissed.

Jiu (Alcoholic Beverages)

It is in my nature not to drink. And since I am strict and discerning in what I consume, I have in turn gained a deep understanding and knowledge of the flavors of *jiu*. Today, Shaoxing is ubiquitous all the way from the sea to deep inland, but considering the delicate freshness of Cang *jiu*, the cool purity of Xun *jiu*, the fresh sweetness of Chuan *jiu*: how could they be ranked lower than Shaoxing! In general, *jiu* could be compared to an old and aged Confucian scholar: the older, the more precious. That from a freshly opened jar is the best, as indicated by the proverb "*Jiu* heads, tea feet."[9]

When the beverage is inadequately warmed, however, it will taste too cool; if too warm, it will taste weak and flavorless; and when warmed too close to the flames, its flavors will change. For the best results, one should warm it by simmering it in water, carefully covering the opening of the warming vessel where the vapors could escape. I have chosen the more drinkable alcoholic beverages and listed them below.

Jintan Yu Jiu (Golden Jar *Jiu* from the Yu Family)

This is made in the household of [Grand Councilor] Yu Minzhong. There are two types: sweet and astringent, with the astringent one

---

9 This may mean that aged *jiu* is best when the jar is just cracked open (like a very old vintage port), and tea is better nearer to its end (when the tea leaf has fully opened up).

being the better. It is so incredibly delicate and refreshing that the sensations go straight to one's bones. Its colors are that of pine flowers, and its flavors are similar to Shaoxing but much cooler and fresher.

Dezhou Lu *Jiu*

This is made in the household of transport officer Lu Yayu. The color is similar to that of most liquor, but its flavors are more concentrated.

Sichuan Pitong *Jiu*

Pitong *jiu* is thoroughly refreshing and cool. It is so much like drinking pear juice or sugar cane juice that one could mistake it for not being *jiu* at all. It is brought in from Wanli in Sichuan Province, and thus it is rare to find ones that have not changed flavor. I have drunk Pitong *jiu* seven times, but the one I had on the raft of Prefecture Governor Yang Lihu was the best.

Shaoxing *Jiu*

In the West, this is still more commonly known (although inaccurately) as Shaoxing "wine."

Shaoxing *jiu* is like an upright and incorruptible official, unadulterated with not a shred of fakery, with a flavor that is authentic and true. It is also like a renowned scholar or mature warrior, who through their long lives have thoroughly examined and experienced everything the world has to offer, thus attaining a complex and substantial character. Shaoxing with water mixed in does not last more than five years, as such, that which has been aged for less than five years should not be drunk.[10] I often refer to Shaoxing as a "renowned scholar" and to distilled liquors as "thugs."

---

10 By avoiding Shaoxing *jiu* less than five years old, one also avoids adulterated Shaoxing *jiu*.

Huzhou Nanxun *Jiu*

Huzhou Nanxun *jiu* has a flavor similar to Shaoxing *jiu* but is much more refreshing and piquant. That which has been aged more than three years is the best.

Changzhou Lanling *Jiu*

In the Tang poems there is a passage that goes "Lanling's fair *jiu*, thickly fragrant and golden bright. Held in a jade bowl, shimmering amber light."[11] I have traveled through Changzhou and drank a *jiu* aged for eight years with Liu Lun. It indeed had the brightness of amber, but its flavor was far too concentrated and no longer had that desired long-lasting refreshing flavor. Yixing city has a Shu mountain *jiu* that is similar to Lanling.

As for *jiu* from Wuxi, it is made from the water of the second-best spring under heaven; as such, it should be one of the best *jiu*. But because it was made improperly by the city's business folk, it had been completely watered down and diluted in quality, which is especially regrettable. It is said that there is still good *jiu* there, but I have yet to try it.

Liyang Black Rice *Jiu*

I almost never drink. Nevertheless, in the year *bingxu* [1766] at the abode of Auditor Ye in Lishui, I drank sixteen cups of their black rice *jiu*, which greatly shocked those around me. All of them pleaded with me to stop. Even though I was wrecking my composure, I could not control myself and put my hand down. Its color was black, with a sweet and fresh flavor that was so incredible that I cannot describe it.

It is told by the traditions of Lishui, that when a daughter is born, one must make a large jar of this *jiu* using the fresh milled

---

11 This line comes from the poem "A Traveler's Journey" 客中行 by the famous Tang dynasty poet Li Bai 李白.

rice of the utmost quality.[12] It is only on the day of the daughter's wedding that the *jiu* is drunk. This means that this kind of *jiu* has been aged at the very least for fifteen or sixteen years. When the lid is cracked open,[13] there is only half a jar of the aged *jiu* left. Its texture is sticky on one's lips and its aroma can be smelled from outside the room.

Suzhou Aged Sanbai *Jiu*

In the thirtieth year of Qianlong [1765], I was in Suzhou having a drink at the home of Zhou Mu'an. The *jiu* I had there was sweet and fair, and stuck to one's lips when drunk. Even when one's cup was filled to the brim, it still does not spill. After I had fourteen cups of it, I still did not know what *jiu* it was, so I asked the master of the house, who replied, "It is a Sanbai *jiu* that has been aged for more than ten years." Since I loved it so much, the next day he gifted me a jar, but it was an entirely different thing. Why must it be?! Indeed, it is hard to acquire the choice items of this world in any quantity. In his annotation of the *Rites of Zhou*, Zheng Kangcheng defined the term *angqi* as: "The jar's content is old and cloudy white. Similar to modern Zanbai." I suspect that this was the *jiu* being referred to.

Nüzhen may refer to the fruit or berries of the privet tree (*Ligustrum lucidum*), known in Traditional Chinese Medicine as *nüzhen zi* 女楨子. An alternate interpretation is the widely practiced tradition of keeping *jiu* when a daughter is born, called *Nüzhen jiu* 女貞酒 (daughter's innocence *jiu*).

Jinhua *Jiu*

Jinhuan *jiu* has the freshness of Shaoxing without its astringency, it has the sweetness of nüzhen without the unrefined characteristics. Like other *jiu*, it is also best when aged. All this is true because the water running by Jinhua is clear and clean.

---

12 These jars are sold by their empty weight. A small one generally weighs around five kg, the larger ones up to fifty kg. A typical jar, which comes up to one's thigh, is around twenty-five kg.

13 The large jars are sealed with layers of lotus leaf, an earthenware top, and capped with a layer of clay and plaster.

Shanxi *Fen Jiu* (Sorghum Liquor)[14]

If one is already drinking *shaojiu* [burnt liquor],[15] choose the more vicious since they are the best. And out of all *shaojiu*, *fen jiu* is the most vicious. I have referred to *shaojiu* as "thugs among men" and "cruel officials in the counties." But for holding fights in an arena, one cannot be without thugs, and to rid a region of bandits, one cannot be without cruel county officials; likewise, to drive out the chills and clear one's bodily stagnation, one cannot be without *shaojiu*. Ranked just behind *Fen jiu* is Shandong *gaoliang* (shorgum) liquor.[16] It can be stored for ten years, whereupon the liquor will turn green in color and becomes sweet in the mouth upon drinking. Just like thugs who have aged; they lose their violent temper and become more amicable. I often see Tong Ershu's household, infusing ten *jin* of *shaojiu* with four *liang* of gojiberries, two *liang* of atractylodes rhizhome,[17] and one *liang* of mulberry root,[18] all wrapped in a cloth. When the jar is opened a month later, the aroma is incredible. When eating pig's head, sheep's tail, salted pork, and the like, one cannot go without *shaojiu*, with each component providing its own benefits.

---

14 *Fen jiu* 汾酒 is a sorghum-based distilled liquor from Shanxi Province. Its name comes from the Fen River near the center of the modern province, a region known in the past as the Fen Prefecture (*Fenzhou* 汾州). The liquor has a long history, tracing back to the Northern and Southern Dynasties Period (420–589 CE). Its first mention is in the Tang dynasty *Book of Northern Qi* (*Bei Qi Shu* 北齊書, Scroll 11). Several Song dynasty works—including the *Northern Mountain Book of Alcoholic Drinks* (*Beishan Jiu Jing* 北山酒經) and the *Manual on Alcoholic Drinks* (*Beipu* 酒譜)—describe it as being a distilled drink produced using a dry-brewing process, indicating the early development of this particular brewing technique used in many types of Chinese alcoholic drinks and vinegars. It was a highly regarded drink during the Tang dynasty—often diluted with water, though that custom ended in the Song dynasty.

15 "Burnt (or roasted) liquor" (*shaojiu* 燒酒) is a term used for all types of distilled grain (e.g. sorghum) liquor. Interestingly, Brandy takes its name from the German *Branntwein*, which also means "burned wine." Vodka and whiskey would also fall in this category. The term *baijiu* 白酒 or "white liquor" is also commonly used to refer to distilled grain liquor, alluding to its colorless clarity—which contrasts with *huangjiu*, or "yellow liquor," which is a brewed, un-distilled alcoholic beverage with a color ranging from light to dark brown.

16 Sorghum (*gaoliang* 高粱) is a plant from the same taxonomic tribe as maize and sugarcane. They all grow well under hot and dry conditions. For this reason, sorghum is often cultivated in northern China and used to supplement rice and wheat flour. It is also widely grown on land that is too dry, sandy, or otherwise unsuitable to cultivate rice or wheat.

17 The rhizome of *Atractylodes lancea* (*cangshu* 蒼术) is a species of plant from the sunflower family.

18 Mullberry root (*bayitian* 巴戟天) is the root portion of *Morinda officinalis*. Commonly known as Indian mulberry, it is from the same family as the coffee plant and the madder dye plant.

Other than that, Suzhou's *nüzhen*, Fuqi's Yuanzao, Xuanzhou's bean *jiu*,[19] and Tongzhou's Red Jujube *jiu* are all subpar and unworthy of consideration. Like Yangzhou flowering quince,[20] they taste crass and vulgar.

---

19 Beans and other pulses are often included in the grain starter of distilled liquors known as *Daqu* liquor, with the most famous one being Maotai. *Daqu* translates as "great starter" and consists of large compressed bricks of ground grains and pulses that have been inoculated with a complex mix of yeast and fungi. The microorganism breaks down the starches and proteins in the grains into sugars and amino acids, which themselves ferment into ethanol and produce a wide variety of fragrance compounds. The *Daqu* starter is added in large quantities to a steamed grain, such as sorghum or rice, and then allowed to ferment before being distilled to produce the final liquor. One of the more popular bean liquors is mung bean liquor (*lüdou jiu* 綠豆酒), and since Xuanzhou is located in Anhui province, well-known for producing said mung bean liquor, the Xuanzhou bean liquor mentioned here is probably something like it.

20 This is likely a liquor made or flavored with the flowering quince. The Chinese term for this fruit is *mugua* 木瓜 or "wood melon." In modern times, *mugua* could either mean a type of quince or a papaya, depending on the region. In inland China, as well as in classical Chinese texts, *mugua* refers almost exclusively to the fruit of the species of flowering quince (*Chaenomeles speciose*) or the Chines quince (*Pseudocydonia sinensis*). These are the types of *mugua* used in Traditional Chinese Medicine, described in detail in Li Shizhen's *Compendium of Materia Medica*. In the tropical and subtropical parts of China, as well as in areas around the world inhabited by the Chinese diaspora where quinces are seldom found, *mugua* almost always refers to the papaya plant (*Carica papaya*). Both plants produce round, elongated, melon-like fruits that grow out of the main trunk or branches of the tree. To disambiguate these two completely different plant and fruits, quinces are known as *xuan mugua* 宣木瓜, or "nobly-proclaimed" melon, and papaya is called *fan mugua* 番木瓜, the "southeast foreigners'" melon.

About the Author

Yuan Mei was born on 25 March 1716 in the Zhejiang provincial capital Hangzhou, to a once eminent family that had fallen on hard times. Yuan's mother had to work to help the family survive, and he was coddled by his grandmother and a widowed aunt, who began to teach him classical literature. He attended several academies and had different mentors. At age twenty-three, Yuan Mei achieved the presented scholar degree (*jinshi* 进士), which won him the patronage of Yin Jishan 尹继善 (1696–1771), an influential Manchu official whose love of literature would make him a lifelong friend and supporter.

In 1742, Yuan Mei passed the palace examinations in Beijing, and started a government career that would take him to positions in Lishui 溧水 (southeast of Nanjing), Jiangpu 江浦 (across the Yangtze River from Nanjing), Shuyang 沭阳 (northern Jiangsu Province), Xi'an (Shaanxi Province), and eventually back to Nanjing. In 1748, Yuan Mei bought a garden villa in Nanjing, north of the city wall, which had suffered neglect before Yuan restored its walls, pavilions, halls, and kiosks. He moved there permanently in 1755, naming it Suiyuan 随园, or Garden of Contentment (or Ease). The name both played on the surname of the villa's original owner and conveyed the idea that one should live life following the patterns of nature and destiny rather than rigidly adhering to preconceived notions and social convention.

Yuan Mei had not worked long enough in government to accumulate the funds necessary to support his family and maintain his garden villa, but his poems, essays, and stories were in great demand. After he compiled and printed his collected works, the income he made from their sale alone may have equaled or surpassed his earlier income as an official. Equally popular and sales-worthy were his textbooks on how to write successful examination essays. Yuan Mei's calligraphy was also prized by connoisseurs. Yuan Mei's wealth permitted him to transform his Garden of Contentment into one of the great garden villas of the age. One of his poet friends claimed that Yuan's garden was the model for the Jia 賈 family garden described so wonderfully by Cao Xueqin 曹雪芹 (c. 1724–c. 1766) in his famous eighteenth-century novel, *Dream of the Red Chamber* (*Honglou meng*红楼梦). Paintings of the Garden of Contentment were copied in the early nineteenth century and one survives in the collection of the Nanjing Museum. Woodblock prints of the garden inspired by those paintings reveal that, following custom, Yuan Mei made the Garden of Contentment into a microcosm of many different worlds in miniature.

At its center was the "World of Poetry," a pavilion where Yuan Mei stacked all the manuscripts of poetry submitted to him by authors from the four corners of the empire. At the western end of the garden was a corridor he called "Poetry Wall," where Yuan pasted thousands of poems presented to him by the famous poets of eighteenth-century China. Yuan had over the years become a strong advocate of education for women and of the qualities of the poetry written by them. In 1796, Yuan compiled an anthology entitled A *Selection of the Poems of the Female Disciples of the Garden of Contentment* (*Suiyuan nü dizi shixuan* 随园女弟子诗选), which contains the work of nineteen women.

To the northwest was the library that housed Yuan Mei's 300,000-volume collection of books. Adjacent to that was the "Repository of Bronze and Stone Objects." We know from references in his poetry that Yuan owned Shang and Zhou dynasty bronze vessels, Tang and Song dynasty ink stones, and Han dynasty bronze mirrors. By his own account, Yuan Mei was crazy about mirrors. He had thousands of them and expressed delight at how, in the evening, they reflected the light from the candles and lamps placed throughout the garden. Nearby was his "World of Glass," whose windows were made of stained glass imported from Europe.

Yuan Zuzhi 袁祖志, one of Yuan Mei's grandsons, noted that, "Furniture was arranged in twenty-three rooms. Aside from the furniture pieces made entirely of Yunnan marble, there were many other pieces inlaid with mother-of-pearl, and other precious materials. Most of the furniture was made of sandalwood, padauk wood, and *nanmu* 楠木 [a hardwood similar to teak]." As did other eighteenth-century collectors, Yuan Mei took great pride in his Ming dynasty porcelains. Even though he was a famous host, he advised against setting a banquet table with serving pieces made during the fifteenth and sixteenth centuries because they might break. "It would be best in the end to use the porcelains fired during our own Qing dynasty, which I feel are already quite elegant and beautiful."

This last quotation comes from the first chapter of Yuan Mei's culinary treaty, *The Way of Eating*, which he compiled over several years with the help of his household chefs. It is replete with advice on what to look for in good soy sauce and where to buy the best vinegar. Yuan offers the following advice on preparing for dinner guests: "Invite people three days in advance of a planned dinner. That way there will be ample time to prepare all the delicacies. If a guest arrives unexpectedly, however, there is nothing to do but serve him what can be made quickly. If you find it necessary to prepare a dish in a hurry, then sauté such things as chicken slices, shredded pork, shrimp meat, *doufu* [tofu], and wine-marinated fish, or ham cured in tea leaves. Demonstrating skill even when forced to prepare a dish in a hurry is something a good cook must know how to do."

Though Yuan accumulated considerable wealth during the decades following his retirement from official service, his life otherwise was a mix of good and bad fortune. Many of his family members passed prematurely, and in 1771, Yuan's old friend and patron Yin Jishan died. On the other hand, he celebrated his mother's ninetieth birthday in 1774 and his own sixtieth in 1775. And in 1778, at sixty-two years old, Yuan Mei finally fathered a son with one of his concubines. Because the boy was born when Yuan was already entering old age, he named him Chi迟, which means "late or slow in arriving."

Yuan Mei died in 1798. Yuan Zuzhi noted in his memoirs: "My grandfather once said, 'After my life is over if you get to hold on to the Garden of Ease [Contentment] for thirty years, then my wishes will be satisfied.' In 1853, the Cantonese bandits sacked Nanjing and the garden was destroyed." Yuan Zuzhi is referring to the Taiping Rebellion (1850–1864), who initially used the villa as a government office but later tore it down and removed all of its contents. Yuan Mei's library was destroyed along with his collection of famous paintings, calligraphy, and the printing blocks for his collected works. Although Yuan Mei would have been pleased that the Garden of Contentment survived as long as it did, the total destruction of his home would have been hard to imagine.

This biography is an abridged version of Prof. Jeffrey Riegel's article on Yuan Mei, published in the *Berkshire Dictionary of Chinese Biography* (2014, vol.3, pp. 1226-1240).

Glossary

Abalone (*baoyu* 鮑魚) are marine sea snails. Fresh abalone can be grilled or steamed and eaten straight out of the shell. When they come in dried form, they need to be cooked for a long time in order to soften them.

Autumn sauce (*qiuyou* 秋油) is a high-quality soy sauce made by filling ceramic vats with soy-sauce mash and exposing those to the full sun in hot summer weather. It is pressed only in late autumn, hence its name. The exposure to the sun supposedly enhances the savory (or umami) taste and gives the autumn sauce its clarity, deep red color, complex flavor, and long shelf-life not found in regular soy sauce. A detailed account on autumn sauce is mentioned in the Qing dynasty work *Manual for Gastronomy from the Suixi Studio* 隨息居飲食譜.

B*aihua* liquor (*baihua jiu* 百花酒) is a fermented rice wine produced in Jiangsu Province since the Northern and Southern Dynasties (420–589 CE). It is known for its alluring fragrance and complex combination of sweet, sour, bitter, and spicy tastes.

Bamboo shoots (*sun* 筍) are the developing shoots of bamboo harvested either before or just after they have broken through the soil. The textures and flavors of bamboo shoots vary widely and range from crisp and sweet, tender and bland, to tough and bitter. Each type varies in method of production, use, preparation, and pricing.

B*ao* (explosive) stir-fry (*bao* 爆) is a cooking technique using very high temperatures. The ingredients are rapidly tossed and seared to completion. When executed correctly, the food has the strong, alluring flavor of broiled and grilled foods known in Cantonese cuisine as ***wokhei***.

Bean starch (*doufen* 豆粉). The Chinese word literally means "bean flour," which could refer to mung bean starch, mung bean flour, roasted soybean powder, or raw soybean powder.

Bing 餅 is any flour- or starch-based dough item that is flattened, usually disk shaped. They can be thicker than an inch or as thin as a sheet of paper and range from a few centimeters to a meter in diameter. They can be filled with savory or sweet ingredients, though the dough itself is usually plain. Although *bing* can be translated to English as "(pan)cake" or "biscuit," the better equivalent term is actually the French word "galette," since it's made of the same ingredients and used to describe a range of dough foods of the same size, form, and flavor.

Bird's nests (*yanwo* 燕窩) are constructed by the swift species *Aerodramus maximus* and *Aerodramus fuciphagus* as they progressively layer their saliva into a crescent-shaped half-bowl form. Raw bird's nests are firm but friable, and although they consist mainly of the dried saliva protein, they still contain feathers and specks of dust that require thorough cleaning prior to preparation.

Celtuce (*wosun* 窩筍) is a Chinese variety of lettuce bred and grown for its thick crunchy stem (*Lactuca sativa* var. *Asparagina*).

Chrysanthemum-pattern cut. See **lychee-pattern cut**.

Clear cooking (*qingdun* 清燉) or clear braising indicates braising food in clear water or broth over a small flame or by steaming. The method emphasizes light flavors and could be considered bland or under-seasoned by those not used to it. It is usually reserved for medicines or food with restorative properties.

Cup (*bei* 杯). There is no direct evidence of how big a cup was, much less what the volumes for more specific cups were, such as that of a "wine cup" (*jiubei* 酒杯) or "tea cup" (*chabei* 茶杯). They were certainly not the same size as the American standard cup (236 ml). Related measurements during the Qing dynasty were the *ge* 合 (103.54 ml) and a *shao* 勺 (scoop, 10.35 ml). Estimates would be around 100 ml for a regular cup, and 30 to 50 ml for a wine cup.

Douchi 豆豉 is a fermented and dried soybean product made by steaming soybeans, allowing them to ferment (using *Aspergillus oryzae* or *Mucor* spp.), salting, and drying them. This is possibly the oldest fermented soybean product. It is also used to make a very high-quality soy sauce in Taiwan known as *yinyou* 蔭油 (lit. shaded sauce).

Dough sauce (*mian jiang* 麵醬, or *tianmian* sauce) is a sweet and salty sauce made primarily from steamed wheat dough, with the occasional addition of soybeans. It is fermented in the same manner as soy sauce. It is used for seasoning meat and tofu dishes or as a dip for vegetables. It is also the sauce served with slices of Peking duck that are wrapped in flat pancakes. In modern Chinese cuisine, a fermented chili bean sauce (*doubanjiang* 豆瓣醬) is often used instead of dough sauce.

Dry stir-fry (*ganchao* 乾炒) is a technique uses oil but adds no additional water or other liquid during the cooking process. It results in stronger fried and caramelized flavors.

Eight treasures (*babao* 八寶). The eight treasures originally referred to Buddhist attributes or signs that symbolize an enlightened mind. In cuisine, eight-treasure dishes range from savory appetizers and main dishes to sweet desserts, but they all contain (roughly) eight different, colorful, flavorful, distinctive, and sometimes expensive ingredients. The number eight (*ba* 八) is an auspicious number because it sounds similar to the word for "becoming wealthy" (*fa* 发).

Five flavors (*wu wei* 五味). The Chinese five flavors are pungent (*xin* 辛), salty (*xian* 咸), sour (*suan* 酸), bitter (*ku* 苦), and sweet (*gan* 甘). These correspond to the five Daoist elements: metal, water, wood, fire, and earth. See also text box on page XXX.

Floss (*song* 鬆) is a dried meat product made by continuously mashing and dry stir-frying seasoned fish, pork, beef, or other meat until the fibers have separated and dried. This results in a soft yet crisp texture resembling wool. It is a favorite of young and old alike as a condiment for rice and the perfect beer snack. Restaurants nowadays also serve it wrapped in lettuce leaves to be eaten like a taco.

Flying flour (*feimian* 飛麵) is a finely milled or sifted wheat flour, similar to modern-day white wheat flour. This is in contrast to more traditional wheat flours that are often stone-ground, which are still commonly used for traditional breads such as chapatis or rustic pastas. Modern mills produce flying flour by first separating out the bran and germ of the wheat kernels, then grinding the starchy wheat endosperm into semolina by crushing it through steel rollers. The ground semolina flour is then ground and refined by multiple cycles of sifting, using sieves with the aid of blown air.

Gan 甘 (sweet or pleasant flavor) is one of the five traditional Chinese flavors. It is an old Chinese word that has been used since Neolithic periods to describe a wide range of pleasant flavors and tastes. It is still used today to communicate the more subtle pleasant tastes. It is used in conjunction with other words to describe pleasant activities and experiences and is incorporated as a radical in several Chinese characters, such as tangerines (*gan* 柑), drunkenness (*han* 酣), and of course, sweet (*tian* 甜).

Gao 糕 is a cake or pudding-like dish. See the text box on page XXX.

Garlic chives (*jiucai* 韭菜) are the leaves from the plant *Allium tuberosum*, which have a strong garlicky and onion-like odor but taste mellow and sweet when cooked. This prolific and hardy perennial is one of the few ancient vegetables that is still commonly grown and used in Chinese cuisine.

Geng 羹 refers to a thick soup or stew. Its history extends back to the Zhou or possibly even the Shang dynasty. It is one of the oldest Chinese food words found on ancient bronze vessels of those periods, stating their use in preparing *geng*. The thick texture of *geng* is conferred through the addition of a starch, such as potato, corn, and arrowroot starches, which give the otherwise textureless broth a silky body. The thick texture, rich umami flavor, and the delicateness of its broth make *geng* an excellent comfort food.

Gui 簋 is a type of double-handled, ceremonial vessel with the form of a round soup tureen on top of a thick, typically square platform. It was used in China from the eleventh century BCE until the Zhou dynasty (1045–256 BCE).

Gun 滚 is a unit of time measurement, literally translated as "to roll" or "to boil." Yuan Mei uses this word to describe a short period of time for cooking or (par)boiling ingredients, roughly equivalent to three seconds.

Heat control (*huo hou* 火候) is a term used to describe the process of controlling both the intensity of the cooking heat and the length of time that the food is in contact with the heat. Cooking over a "real" flame is much preferred in Chinese cuisine, because the heat can be regulated more precisely. See also text box on page XXX.

Hibiscus dishes (*furong* 芙蓉) are so named because they are pale in color, with an irregular form and texture, much like the Chinese hibiscus flower. *Furong* dishes typically involve egg but can also use meat or soft tofu, like *douhua*. Perhaps the best-known example is egg foo yong (*furong*).

Hotpot (*huoguo* 火鍋) or chafing dish. In modern Chinese usage, *huoguo* means "hotpot." This cooking and dining experience involves diners immersing pieces of food into a pot of stock boiling in front of diners on a tabletop stove, removing the ingredients, and eating them right away. In Yuan Mei's time, the *huoguo* was more like a modern chafing dish, where precooked food was kept continuously warm.

Household (*jia* 家). Many of Yuan Mei's recipes come from the household of so-and-so. *Jia* is typically translated as "home" or even "family." As knowledge of these recipes likely did not reside with the people mentioned or their family members, but rather with the unrelated cooks or hired helps, the term "household" is a better fit. It includes these nonfamily members who had the skills and knowledge to produce the dishes that Yuan Mei so liked.

Hun 葷 describes thick, strong-smelling flavors, including foods such as meat, pork, and pungent-smelling vegetables, like onions or garlic. These ingredients are considered unacceptable for consumption in Chinese Buddhism. *Hun* is the opposite of *su* (vegetarian). Although religious at its roots, the concept has been absorbed into secular Chinese society.

Incense sticks (*xiang* 香) were used to measure time in premodern China. Depending on their thickness, they can last anywhere from five minutes to more than one or two hours. Based on some of the recipes and methods of preparation Yuan Mei described, an incense stick should be around one hour.

Jiu 酒 describes a range of alcoholic beverages and can be translated as "wine," "beer," or "liquor." Although traditionally often translated as "wine," many scholars have argued against that option, since *jiu* is generally brewed from grain and, thus, technically more akin to beer. In modern Chinese, the various kinds of alcoholic beverages are often indicated by adding to the word *jiu*, e.g., *pijiu* for beer, *putaojiu* (lit. grape alcohol) for wine, or *baijiu* for the typical Chinese grain liquor. See also page XXX for more information.

Laver (*yincai* 紫菜) is a red seaweed of the genus *Porphyra*, typically P. *umbilicalis*.

Lees (*zao* 糟) is a thick paste consisting of the solids left over from the production of rice wine after the wine has been pressed from the fermented mass. It consists of yeast, aspergillus, and loose fiber from the endosperm of the milled rice grains. Due to the fiber, rice-wine lees are quite different from the lees of Western beers and wines, which consist primarily of yeast.

Lees sauce (*zaoyou* 糟油 or *zaolu* 糟卤) is a condiment made by ageing a mixture of wine lees, Shaoxing *jiu*, sugar, salt, and Osmanthus flowers. Traditionally, wine-lees sauce was made by mixing unfiltered rice wine with lees, sesame oil, salt, and seasoning. This seems a bit strange, however, as rice wine and oil do not naturally mix, and there are no emulsifiers to help them do so.

Lifestock (*sheng* 牲). The term *sheng* was used specifically to describe domesticated animals intended for sacrifice to deities or ancestors. In ancient China, domesticated livestock were consider more desirable and valuable than wild game and more suitable as items for sacrifice, as they tended to be more tender, meaty, and less "gamey" than hunted wild animals. This term can simply be translated as "animal"; however, it actually conveys a concept much more specific.

Lychee-pattern cut (*lizhi xing* 荔枝型) is a cutting technique for meat that creates a deep (but not severing) crisscross pattern and causes the meat to "open up" after cooking, resembling chrysanthemum petals or the skin of a lychee.

Lu 卤 (savory liquid) is a salty cooking liquid or refers to the salty juices that come out of steamed food, thus it translation as salty or savory broth. There are stories of restaurants where a pot of this broth (*laolu*) has been continuously used and replenished for generations, boasted about with pride by a restaurant proprietor to show the history and venerated traditions of their establishment. The related term *lu* 滷, used as a verb, means to cook food in a salty liquid or brine, usually soy sauce.

Mala 麻辣 (hot and spicy) is a flavor combination from the Sichuan region combining hot and spicy chili peppers with the fragrant, numbing flavor of Sichuan pepper.

Mantou 饅頭 (steamed bun) are plain leaven wheat bread consisting only of flour, water, and yeast that is cooked by steaming. To create good steamed buns, the dough needs to be kneaded until the air bubbles created by the yeast are extremely fine and held fast by well-developed gluten strands, making the dough shiny white. Next, the dough must be flattened and stretched so that it has a fine grain, and once steamed, it appears as if the bun consists of many small individual threads. After steaming, the *mantou* can be grilled or eaten directly. When these buns are filled, they are called *baozi*.

Men 悶 literally means "to suffocate" or "humid." In Chinese cuisines, it means to let something sit and continue to cook while covered over low heat.

Ni 膩 (greasy; rich tasting) is a term used for foods or ingredients that have heavy, thick flavors and textures, typically meat. The term is also used to describe smooth textures or rich flavors. In modern usage, it describes unpleasant, overly rich or greasy flavors, or even the nauseated feeling one gets after eating these types of food. Controlling the level of *ni* of a dish through seasoning and spices that "cut" the rich odors and flavors is key in Chinese cooking.

Pan-fry (*youjian* 油煎). This technique refers to cooking a piece of food in a relatively small amount of oil in a pan over moderate heat.

Qing 青 (clear, light and delicate tasting) describes a type of food that has light and delicate flavors or a clear appearance. Such foods are typically not weighed down by heavy, strong, or dense flavors.

Qingcai 青菜 refers specifically to varieties of edible mustards of the species *Brassica rapa*. In common usage, however, it applies to any common green leafy vegetable used in Chinese cuisine.

Raw stir-fry (*shengchao* 生炒). In Chinese cooking, it is common to parcook or deep-fry an ingredient before stir-frying it to speed up the stir-frying process and ensure even cooing. When ingredients such as meats need to be raw when stir-fried, the recipe specifically indicates that.

Red cooking (*hongshao* 紅燒) is a cooking technique that involves quickly braising meat or tofu in dark soy sauce, sugar, *jiu*, and sometimes caramel coloring. Ginger, star anise, green onions, and sometimes black cardamom and cinnamon are added to flavor the mix. When the cooking time is prolonged, the technique is called "stewing" (*lu* 滷).

Salted fish (*xiang* 鯗) is typically made from yellow croaker. It is also called *Taixiang* (salted fish from Taizhou).

Shichen 時辰 (hour). A unit of time used in premodern China, equivalent to about two modern hours, sometimes knowns as "Chinese hours." Each day was divided into twelve *shichen*.

Shrimp sauce (*xiayou* 蝦油) or shrimp oil is a soy sauce that has been boiled and aged with shrimp. It has much more umami flavor and is richer than plain soy sauce. *Xiayou* is sometimes used to describe actual oil that is flavored by frying shrimp heads and shells in it.

Sichuan pepper (*jiao* 椒). When used alone, especially in older documents, *jiao* refers to Sichuan pepper (*Zanthoxylum simulans*). In modern Chinese usage, it functions as the English word "pepper," and combined with other words it indicates different tasting spices. For instance, *hujiao* 胡椒 refers to black pepper (*Piper nigram*), and *lajiao* 辣椒 refers to chili peppers (*Capsicum frutescens*). To disambiguate China's original Sichuan pepper from the "newer" peppers, it is now more common to call it *huajiao* 花椒..

Starch (*xian* 纖) is generally used to bind. In modern Chinese, starch is more commonly referred to as *dianfen* 淀粉 rather than the archaic term *xian*, which literally means "smooth" or "delicate." In modern Chinese, the typical term used for thickening a dish with starch is *gou qian* 勾芡.

Sticky rice (*noumi* 糯米) or glutinous rice is a variety of rice that gets a chewy, sticky texture after cooking due to its high amylopectin content. It is commonly used in sweet desserts in numerous East Asian and South East Asian cultures, and in the preparation of festive foods. It is also the preferred type of rice for making rice wine.

Stir-fry (*chao* 炒) is a Chinese cooking technique that involves searing small quantities of ingredients at high temperature while stirring or tossing so that the food is quickly cooked. Trying to stir-fry at lower heat or with larger amounts of food is not possible, since it causes the water in the food to pool instead of evaporate quickly, thus leading to a braised or stewed dish. Stir-frying is sometimes equated with the Western cooking technique "sautéing," which, while similar, is not altogether the same due to the lower heat and speed used.

Su 素 (vegetarian) refers to foods that are acceptable for consumption in Chinese Buddhism, consisting of "light" tasting vegetables and plant products in general. It is the opposite of *hun*.

Sweet dough sauce (*tianmian jiang* 甜麵醬). See **dough sauce** (*mianjiang*).

Sweet sauce (*Tianjiang* 甜醬) is a sweet soy-sauce-based condiment. It could refer to sweet dough sauce (*tianmian jiang* 甜麵醬) or to a sweetened soy sauce similar to Taiwanese thickened soy sauce (*jiang yougao* 醬油膏).

Tender (*su* 酥). The Chinese term *su* translates as "tender," but only in the context of describing baked goods, such as "tender shortbread" or "tender biscuits." This tender food has a firm and solid texture but quickly crumbles and disintegrates when subjected to a slight force.

Texture food is a type of food not eaten for its innate taste or flavor, but rather for its unique texture, be it bouncy, chewy, or rubbery. Preparation of these foods is lengthy and tedious due to the amount of time needed to extract every whiff of odor and shred of taste, then replacing the flavor with chicken or meat broth.

Thirteen Confucian Classics 十三经. The Confucian Classics generally include thirteen traditional philosophical works, including many of the works that Yuan Mei mentions in his preface, such as the *Classic of Changes* (*Yijing* 易經; also known as *the* I-*Ching* or I *Ching*), a book of divination; the *Classic of Documents* (*Shangshu* 尚書; also known as the *Classic of* History or S*hujing* 書經), the *Analects of Confucius* (*Lunyu* 論語), and the *Classic of Rites* (*Liji* 禮記, also known as the *Lijing* 礼经). The other classics are: the *Classic of Poetry* (also known as the *Book of Song*), R*ites of Zhou*, C*eremonies and Rites*, *Zuo Commentary on the Spring and Autumn Annals*, *Gongyang Commentary on the Spring and Autumn Annals*, *Guliang Commentary on the Spring and Autumn Annals*, *Classic of Filial Piety*, E*rya* (a dictionary and encyclopedic work), and the *Mencius* (the writings attributed to the Confucian philosopher Mencius).

Tofu curd (*funao* 腐腦, tofu flower, tofu brain) is the fresh curd used for making tofu, allowed to fully set instead of being ladled into a cloth-lined mold and pressed. Like all tofu, it is made by adding a coagulant such as calcium sulfate to hot soy milk. The texture is so soft, tender, and fragile that one could actually drink it instead of eat it. It is known as "tofu brain" because of this extremely soft texture, and sometimes translated as "tofu flower" (*douhua*) since its fragility causes it to be easily broken into fragments resembling flowers.

Wok (*youguo* 油鍋). The Chinese term literally means "oil pot," but it refers to the utensil used for oil-based cooking often used in Chinese cuisines.

Wokhei (*huoqi* 鑊氣) is a Cantonese term used to describe the flavor of food that has been stir-fried at high temperatures, constantly tossed in the process, and served immediately. The aroma produced in part through the Maillard reaction (protein-sugar pyrolysis) but also in large part thanks to the partial oil combustion. The fact that Western cuisine does not intentionally cook with flaming oil is the reason why one seldom finds strong *wokhei* in Western foods. The exception to this is a well-marbled steak cooked on a hot charcoal grill and eaten right off the grill. Sadly, too many restaurants (and home chefs) rest their meat for so long that any *wokhei* has long dissipated by the time it reaches the table.

Xian 鮮 (savory, umami) is one of the lesser known flavors. It translates as "savory" or "fresh," depending on the context.

Xin 辛 (pungent; sharp, spicy, unpleasant flavor) is an old Chinese word used in modern cuisine to describe a wide range of hot and spicy flavors. It is commonly used with the character *la* 辣 to place further emphasis on the meaning of harsh spiciness. Outside of cuisine, it is also used to describe difficult and toilsome activities (*xinku* 辛苦) or feelings of intense suffering (*xinsuan* 辛酸). Interestingly, the two latter terms also contain the words for bitter (*ku* 苦) and sour (*suan* 酸). The word *xin* has origins in Neolithic Chinese society, signifying a stick-handled knife or blade used for punishing criminals and slaves, with its original meaning describing corporal punishment and the intense pain associated with it. In later dynasties, the term became associated with the sense of taste, describing a gamut of unpleasant flavors, such as the taste of metal (think biting into aluminum foil) or the sharp and hot flavors of plants such as mustard, garlic, and chives.

Yang 羊. Lamb, goat, and mutton are all represented by this word in Chinese.

Zhenjiang vinegar (*Zhenjiang cu* 鎮江醋) is one of the most famous black vinegars in Chinese cuisine, with a deep, complex fragrance unique in the world of vinegars. It gets its name from where it is produced—in Zhenjiang, Jiangsu Province, famous for its wine and, thus not surprisingly, its vinegar. Zhenjiang vinegar is brewed using a dry fermentation method. First, rice wine is brewed, then mixed with large quantities of wheat bran and vinegar starter, which soak up the wine to produce a moist but solid and aerated mass. The mixture is allowed to ferment and age. When the dry mixture is mature, it is eluted with water to extract the vinegar as liquid and further stored and aged prior to sale. The dry fermentation results in the production of numerous aromatic compounds, which contribute to the powerful fragrance of Zhenjiang vinegar.

Zongzi 粽子 are glutinous rice packages wrapped in bamboo leaves. They can have a sweet or savory filling as well. They are eaten during the Duanwu (Dragon Boat) Festival, when the poet and statesmen Qu Yuan is remembered.

Index of Recipes

Index of Ingredients and Terms